Battleground

Battle for the Escaut 1940

Battleground series:

Stamford Bridge & Hastings *by* Peter Marren
Wars of the Roses - Wakefield / Towton *by* Philip A. Haigh
Wars of the Roses - Barnet *by* David Clark
Wars of the Roses - Tewkesbury *by* Steven Goodchild
Wars of the Roses - The Battles of St Albans *by*
Peter Burley, Michael Elliott & Harvey Wilson
English Civil War - Naseby *by* Martin Marix Evans, Peter Burton and Michael Westaway
English Civil War - Marston Moor *by* David Clark
War of the Spanish Succession - Blenheim 1704 *by* James Falkner
War of the Spanish Succession - Ramillies 1706 *by* James Falkner
Napoleonic - Hougoumont *by* Julian Paget and Derek Saunders
Napoleonic - Waterloo *by* Andrew Uffindell and Michael Corum
Zulu War - Isandlwana *by* Ian Knight and Ian Castle
Zulu War - Rorkes Drift *by* Ian Knight and Ian Castle
Boer War - The Relief of Ladysmith *by* Lewis Childs
Boer War - The Siege of Ladysmith *by* Lewis Childs
Boer War - Kimberley *by* Lewis Childs

Mons *by* Jack Horsfall and Nigel Cave
Néry *by* Patrick Tackle
Retreat of I Corps 1914 *by* Jerry Murland
Aisne 1914 *by* Jerry Murland
Aisne 1918 *by* David Blanchard
Le Cateau *by* Nigel Cave and Jack Shelden
Walking the Salient *by* Paul Reed
Ypres - 1914 Messines *by* Nigel Cave and Jack Sheldon
Ypres - 1914 Menin Road *by* Nigel Cave and Jack Sheldon
Ypres - 1914 Langemarck *by* Jack Sheldon and Nigel Cave
Ypres - Sanctuary Wood and Hooge *by* Nigel Cave
Ypres - Hill 60 *by* Nigel Cave
Ypres - Messines Ridge *by* Peter Oldham
Ypres - Polygon Wood *by* Nigel Cave
Ypres - Passchendaele *by* Nigel Cave
Ypres - Airfields and Airmen *by* Mike O'Connor
Ypres - St Julien *by* Graham Keech
Ypres - Boesinghe *by* Stephen McGreal
Walking the Somme *by* Paul Reed
Somme - Gommecourt *by* Nigel Cave
Somme - Serre *by* Jack Horsfall & Nigel Cave
Somme - Beaumont Hamel *by* Nigel Cave
Somme - Thiepval *by* Michael Stedman
Somme - La Boisselle *by* Michael Stedman
Somme - Fricourt *by* Michael Stedman
Somme - Carnoy-Montauban *by* Graham Maddocks
Somme - Pozières *by* Graham Keech
Somme - Courcelette *by* Paul Reed
Somme - Boom Ravine *by* Trevor Pidgeon
Somme - Mametz Wood *by* Michael Renshaw
Somme - Delville Wood *by* Nigel Cave
Somme - Advance to Victory (North) 1918 *by* Michael Stedman
Somme - Flers *by* Trevor Pidgeon
Somme - Bazentin Ridge *by* Edward Hancock
Somme - Combles *by* Paul Reed
Somme - Beaucourt *by* Michael Renshaw
Somme - Redan Ridge *by* Michael Renshaw
Somme - Hamel *by* Peter Pedersen
Somme - Villers-Bretonneux *by* Peter Pedersen
Somme - Airfields and Airmen *by* Mike O'Connor
Airfields and Airmen of the Channel Coast *by* Mike O'Connor
In the Footsteps of the Red Baron *by* Mike O'Connor
Arras - Airfields and Airmen *by* Mike O'Connor
Arras - The Battle for Vimy Ridge *by* Jack Sheldon & Nigel Cave
Arras - Vimy Ridge *by* Nigel Cave
Arras - Gavrelle *by* Trevor Tasker and Kyle Tallett
Arras - Oppy Wood *by* David Bilton
Arras - Bullecourt *by* Graham Keech
Arras - Monchy le Preux *by* Colin Fox
Walking Arras *by* Paul Reed
Hindenburg Line *by* Peter Oldham
Hindenburg Line - Epehy *by* Bill Mitchinson
Hindenburg Line - Riqueval *by* Bill Mitchinson
Hindenburg Line - Villers-Plouich *by* Bill Mitchinson
Hindenburg Line - Cambrai Right Hook *by* Jack Horsfall & Nigel Cave
Hindenburg Line - Cambrai Flesquières *by* Jack Horsfall & Nigel Cave
Hindenburg Line - Saint Quentin *by* Helen McPhail and Philip Guest
Hindenburg Line - Bourlon Wood *by* Jack Horsfall & Nigel Cave

Cambrai - Airfields and Airmen *by* Mike O'Connor
Aubers Ridge *by* Edward Hancock
La Bassée - Neuve Chapelle *by* Geoffrey Bridger
Loos - Hohenzollern Redoubt *by* Andrew Rawson
Loos - Hill 70 *by* Andrew Rawson
Fromelles *by* Peter Pedersen
The Battle of the Lys 1918 *by* Phil Tomaselli
Accrington Pals Trail *by* William Turner
Poets at War: Wilfred Owen *by* Helen McPhail and Philip Guest
Poets at War: Edmund Blunden *by* Helen McPhail and Philip Guest
Poets at War: Graves & Sassoon *by* Helen McPhail and Philip Guest
Gallipoli *by* Nigel Steel
Gallipoli - Gully Ravine *by* Stephen Chambers
Gallipoli - Anzac Landing *by* Stephen Chambers
Gallipoli - Suvla August Offensive *by* Stephen Chambers
Gallipoli - Landings at Helles *by* Huw & Jill Rodge
Walking the Gallipoli *by* Stephen Chambers
Walking the Italian Front *by* Francis Mackay
Italy - Asiago *by* Francis Mackay
Verdun: Fort Douamont *by* Christina Holstein
Verdun: Fort Vaux *by* Christina Holstein
Walking Verdun *by* Christina Holstein
Verdun: The Left Bank *by* Christina Holstein
Zeebrugge & Ostend Raids 1918 *by* Stephen McGreal

Germans at Beaumont Hamel *by* Jack Sheldon
Germans at Thiepval *by* Jack Sheldon

SECOND WORLD WAR

Dunkirk *by* Patrick Wilson
Calais *by* Jon Cooksey
Boulogne *by* Jon Cooksey
Saint-Nazaire *by* James Dorrian
Walking D-Day *by* Paul Reed
Atlantic Wall - Pas de Calais *by* Paul Williams
Atlantic Wall - Normandy *by* Paul Williams
Normandy - Pegasus Bridge *by* Carl Shilleto
Normandy - Merville Battery *by* Carl Shilleto
Normandy - Utah Beach *by* Carl Shilleto
Normandy - Omaha Beach *by* Tim Kilvert-Jones
Normandy - Gold Beach *by* Christopher Dunphie & Garry Johnson
Normandy - Gold Beach Jig *by* Tim Saunders
Normandy - Juno Beach *by* Tim Saunders
Normandy - Sword Beach *by* Tim Kilvert-Jones
Normandy - Operation Bluecoat *by* Ian Daglish
Normandy - Operation Goodwood *by* Ian Daglish
Normandy - Epsom *by* Tim Saunders
Normandy - Hill 112 *by* Tim Saunders
Normandy - Mont Pinçon *by* Eric Hunt
Normandy - Cherbourg *by* Andrew Rawson
Normandy - Commandos & Rangers on D-Day *by* Tim Saunders
Das Reich – Drive to Normandy *by* Philip Vickers
Oradour *by* Philip Beck
Market Garden - Nijmegen *by* Tim Saunders
Market Garden - Hell's Highway *by* Tim Saunders
Market Garden - Arnhem, Oosterbeek *by* Frank Steer
Market Garden - Arnhem, The Bridge *by* Frank Steer
Market Garden - The Island *by* Tim Saunders
Rhine Crossing – US 9th Army & 17th US Airborne *by* Andrew Rawson
British Rhine Crossing – Operation Varsity *by* Tim Saunders
British Rhine Crossing – Operation Plunder *by* Tim Saunders
Battle of the Bulge – St Vith *by* Michael Tolhurst
Battle of the Bulge – Bastogne *by* Michael Tolhurst
Channel Islands *by* George Forty
Walcheren *by* Andrew Rawson
Remagen Bridge *by* Andrew Rawson
Cassino *by* Ian Blackwell
Anzio *by* Ian Blackwell
Dieppe *by* Tim Saunders
Fort Eben Emael *by* Tim Saunders
Crete – The Airborne Invasion *by* Tim Saunders
Malta *by* Paul Williams
Bruneval Raid *by* Paul Oldfield
Cockleshell Raid *by* Paul Oldfield

Battleground Europe

Battle for the Escaut 1940

The France and Flanders Campaign

Jerry Murland

Series Editor
Nigel Cave

Pen & Sword
MILITARY

First published in Great Britain in 2016 by
Pen & Sword Military
An imprint of
Pen & Sword Books Ltd
47 Church Street
Barnsley
South Yorkshire
S70 2AS

Copyright © Jerry Murland, 2016

ISBN 978 147385 261 7

The right of Jerry Murland to be identified as Author of this work has been asserted by him in accordance with the Copyright, Designs and Patents Act 1988.

A CIP catalogue record for this book is available from the British Library.

All rights reserved. No part of this book may be reproduced or transmitted in any form or by any means, electronic or mechanical including photocopying, recording or by any information storage and retrieval system, without permission from the Publisher in writing.

Typeset in Times New Roman by Chic Graphics

Printed and bound in England by
CPI Group (UK) Ltd., Croydon, CR0 4YY

Pen & Sword Books Ltd incorporates the imprints of
Pen & Sword Archaeology, Atlas, Aviation, Battleground, Discovery, Family History, History, Maritime, Military, Naval, Politics, Railways, Select, Social History, Transport, True Crime, Claymore Press, Frontline Books, Leo Cooper, Praetorian Press, Remember When, Seaforth Publishing and Wharncliffe.

For a complete list of Pen & Sword titles please contact
PEN & SWORD BOOKS LIMITED
47 Church Street, Barnsley, South Yorkshire, S70 2AS, England
E-mail: enquiries@pen-and-sword.co.uk
Website: www.pen-and-sword.co.uk

Contents

List of Maps vi
Introduction by the Series Editor vii
Author's Introduction ix
Acknowledgements xii

Chapter One	**First Steps to War** 1	
Chapter Two	**III Corps on the Escaut** 12	
Chapter Three	**II Corps on the Escaut** 32	
Chapter Four	**I Corps on the Escaut** 44	
Chapter Five	**Artillery on the Escaut** 59	
Chapter Six	**The Tours** 67	
	Car Tour 1	**Oudenaarde to Elsegem** 71
	Car Tour 2	**Kaster to Escanaffles** 88
	Car Tour 3	**Helkijn to Tournai** 101
	Car Tour 4	**Chercq to Warnaffles Farm** 121
	Walk 1	**Pecq and Poplar Ridge** 138
	Walk 2	**Hollain** 147

Appendix 156
Selected Bibliography 157
Index 158

List of Maps

The Escaut – 16-22 May 1940.	viii
A map depicting the positions of the 1/5 and 1/6 Queens on the Escaut. Taken from *The History of The Queen's Royal Regiment Vol VIII 1924-1948*.	15
A map of the East Surrey deployment on the Escaut taken from the *History of the East Surrey Regiment Vol IV*.	25
A map from the *History of the Duke of Cornwall's Light Infantry 1939-1945* depicting the sector from Brugge to Escanaffles showing the location of the Rijtgracht.	27
A map taken from *The Grenadier Guards in the War of 1939-1945* depicting the positions of the Grenadier and Coldstream Guards around Pecq.	41
A map taken from *The History of the Royal Warwickshire Regiment* showing the location of the three Royal Warwickshire battalions.	52
A sketch map drawn by Captain Eric Jones depicting the 2/Gloucester's deployment at Bruyelle.	56
Walk 1 – map of the ground south of Pecq.	139
Walk 2 – map of Hollain.	148
A map depicting the line of attack followed by the 1/Ox and Bucks Light Infantry on 21 May. Taken from Lieutenant Colonel Whitfeld's account of May 1940.	152

Introduction by Series Editor

It is a great pleasure to write the introduction to this welcome book by Jerry Murland, the first in a series on the BEF's May-June 1940 campaign that, effectively, culminated in the evacuation from the beaches at Dunkirk and along the coast to the southwest. The campaign of 1940 has been rather neglected over the years, overwhelmed by the amount of literature produced, including a range of guides in the *Battleground Europe* series, on the fighting in France and the Low Countries after the D Day landings of June 1944. What has been produced on Britain's contribution in that late spring of 1940 has tended to concentrate on the final days of the Expeditionary Force before its evacuation.

This first book handles the BEF's defence of the Escaut, confronted as its commander, Viscount Gort, was by the devastating onslaught launched by the Germans against a quiescent allied front that had been most notable for its lack of aggressive activity since the declaration of war in September 1939.

A short but very helpful introductory chapter sets the scene for the descriptions of the fighting (that effectively only lasted a couple of days from 19 May) that developed along the Escaut – a defence provided by a mixture of regular and territorial troops who were generally inadequately equipped for the task, despite the fact that the war had been in progress for over eight months. Hitler's infamous Halt Order of 24 May, shortly after the withdrawal from the Escaut, to allow Kleist's armoured corps to consolidate came to the rescue of the BEF, almost certainly saving it from utter destruction.

What makes this book stand out is the large (over fifty percent of the book) section devoted to touring the Escaut area, supplementing the full narrative of this short-lived defensive action. It is to be hoped that the books in the series will provoke greater interest in the often heroic actions of the various units in the startlingly short (when compared to the impasse of the Great War) campaign and bring a new generation to visit the scenes of these confused actions, inevitable when a front was giving way as this was before von Runstedt's Army Group A. Changes in the course of the Escaut, as well as post war reconstruction and subsequent development since that fateful May of 1940, make following the action on the ground potentially difficult, but it is a hazard that Jerry masterfully overcomes.

As well as taking the battlefield tourer to the ground he also provides a guide to the burial places of the fallen, be it in stand alone CWGC cemeteries or in small groups in the various churchyards and communal cemeteries; men who one can legitimately suspect rarely get visited. I, for one, will make sure that I spend some time in honouring their memory.

Nigel Cave, *Ratcliffe College*
August 2016

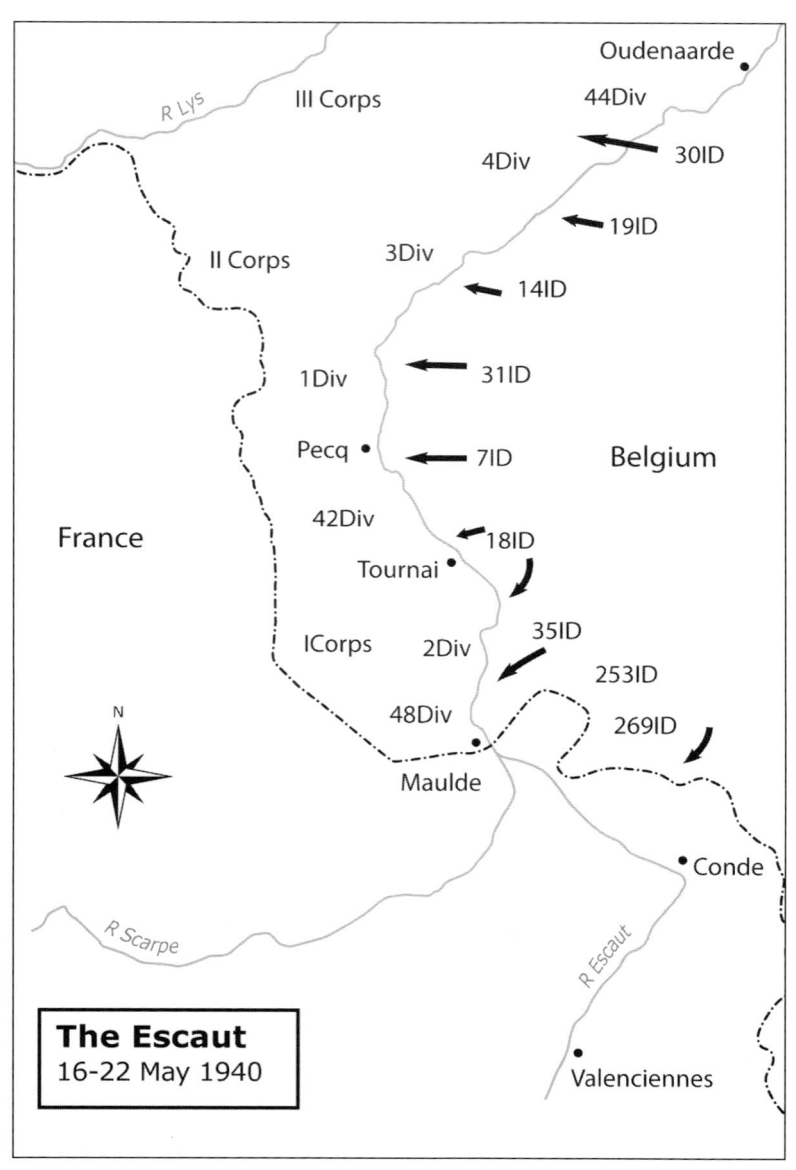

The British sector ran for some thirty miles from Eine, just north of Oudenaarde, through Tournai to Bléharies in the south. The deployment of the British divisions are shown to the west of the river while the attacking German divisions are abbreviated to their divisional numeral followed by ID – Infantry Division.

Author's Introduction

The Escaut is the French name for the River Scheldt, which flows for 270 miles (438 kilometers) from Gouy in the Department of the Aisne across northern France and western Belgium to its estuary in Holland. Contemporary accounts and regimental histories often use the term canal when describing the river, despite the fact that in May 1940 it was more of a meandering river than the canalized waterway we see today. From 19-23 May 1940 the British Expeditionary Force – having retreated from the line of the River Dyle – was defending a thirty mile section of this river from Oudenaarde to Bléharies and was sandwiched in between the Belgian Army to the north and the French First Army to the south. At the time it was perhaps seen as the last real opportunity for the Allied armies to halt the advancing German Army Group B as it raced through Belgium; but in reality the Allied armies were already outflanked, as the Panzer divisions of Army Group A had broken through the Meuse front and were advancing rapidly across France.

For a few days in May 1940 the Escaut provided a temporary military check on the German advance across Belgium. However, although the river line was defended by seven divisions – roughly equating to each battalion defending one mile of winding river bank – there were still gaps in the line as battalions were allocated differing lengths of the river to defend. Added to this was the fall in the level of water in the river, partly due to the opening of the sluices at Valenciennes and aggravated by the lack of rainfall, which inevitably reduced the effectiveness of the Escaut as a barrier. Indeed, as every soldier knows from his training, unless every yard of an obstacle – in this case the river bank and its bridges – is kept under constant surveillance there are inevitably going to be opportunities for enemy forces to cross under cover of darkness or even during the periods of early morning mist; which is exactly what happened in the 44th Divisional sector to the south of Oudenaarde.

For the most part the Escaut was some twenty yards wide and ten feet in depth, with the tow paths in some places ten feet above the water, which in effect obscured any meaningful observation of the last three hundred yards on the opposite bank. Except where the river runs through urban areas, it is bordered by low lying pastures punctuated by small woods and coppices. On the western – British – side of the river there is some higher ground between Anzegem and Knok; but on the eastern side two steep hills – Mont St Aubert and the Mont de l'Enclus – enabled

German observers to overlook the ground almost as far back as the French frontier. Much later in the war these hills were used to discharge V-weapons against England.

However, for the battlefield visitor, the post-war realignment and widening of the river has exacerbated the difficulty in pinpointing exactly where some units were located. This was not assisted by the development and modernization of industrial areas, particularly south of Tournai, which has made some sectors almost unrecognizable from the river frontage that the BEF defended in May 1940. As a consequence some bridging points that are referred to in regimental histories and war diaries of the period are often no longer in existence, while other sectors, such as that at Oudenaarde, are difficult to equate with contemporary descriptions provided by soldiers who fought on the Escaut. It is this factor, together with the short span of time that British units spent defending the western bank, that has made a detailed examination of the Battle on the Escaut more akin to piecing together a jig-saw puzzle.

When describing the fighting I have often referred to modern day road numbering in order to give the reader using current maps of the area a more precise location. While some of the abbreviations in the text are self explanatory, others require a modicum of explanation. I have used a form of abbreviation when describing battalion formations, thus after its first mention in the text the 2nd Battalion Royal Norfolk Regiment becomes the 2/Norfolks or, more simply, the Norfolks.

German army units are a little more complex. Within the infantry regiment there were three battalions – each one approximately the size of a British battalion – and as with their British counterparts the battalion was broken down into four companies of riflemen who were given an Arabic numeral, for example, 3 *Kompanie*. Again, I have abbreviated when describing these units, thus Infantry Regiment 162 becomes IR162, while the second battalion within that regiment is abbreviated to II/IR162. In the same way, German infantry divisions are often referred to in their abbreviated form, hence ID31 refers to the 31st Infantry Division.

The Battle of Oudenaarde 1708

May 1940 was not the first occasion British troops had fought in this area. 250 years previously one of the key engagements of the Spanish Wars of Succession was fought just to the north of Oudenaarde, with British, Dutch, Austrians, Hanoverians, Prussians and Danes pitted against the French and Bavarians. British forces were commanded by John Churchill, the Duke of Marlborough, who fought against the Duke of Burgundy and Marshal Vendôme. Marlborough's army numbered 80,000 men while the French army numbered around 95,000 men. As the opposing armies manoeuvred across Flanders, the French captured Ghent and Bruges and, in late June 1708, moved against the British held Oudenaarde. Beaten on the field of battle the French retired to Ghent, leaving Marlborough the victor. It is thought that the French army lost 15,000 men while the Allies forces are said to have lost fewer than 3000 officers and men. The next morning British and Prussian cavalry resumed the pursuit of the French army and crossed the border into France, reaching the outskirts of Arras. Many of the regiments that fought on the Escaut in 1940 were also present as part of Marlborough's army, notably the Grenadier and Coldstream Guards, the East Kent Regiment (the Buffs), the Gloucesters and Royal Hampshires.

The First World War
The German advance in 1914 saw the Western Front trench lines being established west of the Escaut and, up until late 1918, the area remained in German hands. The American 37th 'Buckeye' Division from Ohio crossed the Escaut at Eine and Huevel on 2 November 1918 and the American 91st Division liberated Oudenaarde during the 'advance to victory' just days before the Armistice was declared, ending the 'war to end all wars'. Further south, Tournai, which had been very badly damaged by air and artillery attacks, was liberated by the 47th (London) and 74th (Yeomanry) Divisions on 8 November 1918.

After Dunkirk and the 1940 campaign, advancing Allied troops were back on the Escaut in September 1944; Oudenaarde was liberated by the British on 5 September – you will find a memorial to the British 7th Division in the Tacambaroplein – and the American First Army arrived at Tournai two days earlier, on 3 September 1944.

Language
Flemish is spoken by some three and a half million people. The population of Belgium is roughly eight million, made up of Flemish speakers in the north, French speaking Walloons in the south and a smaller group in central Belgium who are bi-lingual. The frontier between the Flemish and French speaking populations has not changed since the fifth century and runs from Mousson, just south of Ypres, to Visé, just north of Liège, passing south of Brussels, through the village of Waterloo. Thus, the area covered by this guidebook falls in both French and Flemish speaking areas and battlefield tourists will often find place names on maps written in both Flemish and French. To avoid confusion I have used the Flemish spelling of place names where appropriate but have retained the French name for the river – the Escaut – which is used consistently in The British Official History, *The War in France and Flanders* by Major Lionel Ellis, and by regimental historians and war diarists.

Acknowledgements

Writing a book of this nature not only takes time but involves a considerable amount of walking the ground in order to – as far as possible – provide an accurate summary of what took place in May 1940. Fortunately there are still local individuals who remember the rather fleeting British defence along the Escaut in 1940 and to them I must extend my thanks for their patience in answering my seemingly endless questions. I have also relied on the knowledge and records available to Charles Deligne, the curator of the Tournai Military History Museum and Stijn Lybeet, at the Oudenaarde Museum, to correct my errors and point me in the direction of contemporary maps of the river line. Both these individuals have also been responsible for augmenting my knowledge of the history and development of a part of Belgium that has until now escaped my attention. Other local material that has come my way has been translated from the Flemish by Sabine Declercq – Couwet, to whom I owe a great debt of thanks. My thanks must also go to the sound department at the Imperial War Museum, the National Archives at Kew and the curators and keepers of records at the seemingly endless museums and archives I either visited or contacted. Members of the WW2 Talk Forum have also been extremely helpful in answering my questions and providing me with material as has Laura Dimmock-Jones at the RUSI Library who has my gratitude in assisting me in locating obscure volumes buried in the depths of one of the best military libraries in the country. I am also very grateful to the Holdich Family for allowing me to quote from Neil Holdich's diary and to the Stow Archive for sending me a copy of Captain Dick Tomes' diary, which shed so much light on the Warwickshires' positions in Hollain.

On my first visit to the area in 2014 I was accompanied by Jon Cooksey, whose enthusiasm and knowledge of the 1940 campaign was responsible for my developing interest in the actions of the BEF in the early stages of the Second World War. His good company and liking for Belgian beer is only surpassed by that of Tom Waterer – an individual who questions everything and enjoys walking the battlefields and following the trail of the BEF as they retreated towards Dunkirk and the channel ports. To both these stalwarts I extend my thanks and look forward to many more trips across the water and the discovery of new beers to sample.

While I have made every effort to trace the copyright holders of the material used, I crave the indulgence of literary executors or copyright holders where those efforts have so far failed and would encourage them to contact me through the publisher so that any error can be rectified.

Finally, I must once again thank my wife Joan for her tolerance in putting up with my absence, not only from home when visiting the battlefields and distant archives but my absence from family life when surrounded by mountains of paper and dusty volumes of regimental histories.

Jerry Murland
Coventry 2015

Chapter One

First Steps to War

On 3 September 1939 Neville Chamberlain announced to the nation that Germany's military incursion into Poland on 1 September 1939 had now resulted in a formal declaration of war. His address brought to an end the twenty-one years of uneasy peace that had elapsed since the Armistice of 11 November 1918 ended the First World War. For Chamberlain the declaration of war was also a personal failure, ultimately leading to his resignation eight months later on 10 May, the very day German forces began their offensive into France and Flanders.

Britain's undertaking to have two full army corps assembled in France thirty-three days after mobilization went remarkably smoothly, yet the stark reality of another war with Germany did not begin to surface amongst the British public until after the Munich Crisis of 1936. Rearmament then forced its way into the mindset of a population in which memories of 1914-18 still lingered. It also pushed its way into the political agenda, when the Territorial Army was doubled in size on 29 March by the War Minister, Leslie Hore-Belisha, by requiring each of the existing Territorial Army units to form duplicate units.

Neville Chamberlain is best known for his policy of appeasement.

The British Expeditionary Force

In overall command of the BEF was 53-year-old General Lord Gort. A highly decorated Grenadier Guards officer, he had served in the First World War with some distinction; wounded on four occasions, he had been

Leslie Hore-Belisha was Minister for War in 1939.

decorated with the Military Cross (MC) and the Distinguished Service Order (DSO) and two bars. His award of the coveted Victoria Cross (VC) came whilst he was commanding the 1st Battalion during the battle on the Canal du Nord in 1918. By 1935 he had been promoted to major general and three years later, after a short tenure as Military Secretary to Leslie Hore-Belisha, he was appointed Chief of the Imperial General Staff (CIGS). There is no doubt that his appointment as CIGS had a great deal to do with his war record and Hore-Belisha's misplaced desire for the army to be led by a man of proven courage on the battlefield.

John Vereker, 6th Viscount Gort, Commander in Chief of the BEF.

If Gort's appointment as CIGS was met with a degree of bewilderment, then his subsequent confirmation on 1 September 1939 as Commander-in-Chief of the BEF drew gasps of disbelief, particularly from General Sir Edmund Ironside, who had been confidently expecting command of the BEF and now found himself appointed CIGS in Gort's place. 'The Army was certainly amazed', wrote Major General Bernard Montgomery, and was, 'even more amazed when Ironside was made CIGS in place of Gort.' But despite the barrage of criticism that faced his appointment, it has to be said, whatever his faults may have been, when the situation facing the BEF became desperate in the last days of May, Gort maintained his composure and grasp of the situation.

Edmund Ironside expected to command the BEF in 1939.

I Corps

Even to the relatively unobservant it would have been difficult not to notice that many of the men now landing in France with the BEF were wearing medal ribbons from the previous war, which was certainly the case with the two corps commanders, both of whom were older than Gort and had been senior to him before his recent rise. Commanding I Corps was General Sir John Dill, an individual

Bernard Law Montgomery commanded the 3rd Division in 1940.

who had served with distinction under Douglas Haig, and who many felt had been repeatedly passed over for the top appointments until he succeeded Ironside as CIGS on 27 May 1940. After Dill's recall, command of I Corps was passed to Lieutenant General Michael Barker; an appointment that caused the outspoken Montgomery to remark that, 'only a madman would give a corps to Barker', another comment that was to prove predictive in the dark days ahead. Brigadier Charles Norman, commanding 1/Armoured Reconnaissance Brigade, was no less complimentary and was of the opinion Barker was only given the appointment because he was the next major general on the list, 'but was quite unsuited to command in the field'.

Sir John Dill commanded I Corps until late May 1940.

II Corps

In command of II Corps was the energetic and able Lieutenant General Alan Brooke, a gunner who rose from lieutenant to lieutenant colonel over the four years of the First World War. Brooke was unconvinced of the Allied chances of holding the forthcoming German offensive, an observation that was not held by Gort, who regarded him as too much of a pessimist. Both Brooke and Dill had drawn Gort's attention to the potential weaknesses of an advance into Belgium, views that were seemingly dismissed by the commander-in-chief. Dill is also known to have discussed his fears with the military historian Cyril Falls on his return to England in April 1940, but both men could not have guessed at the speed and ferocity of the German panzer advance.

Alan Brooke commanded II Corps in 1940.

The BEF frontage in France took the form of a forty-five mile long salient formed by the Franco-Belgian frontier, with its left flank on Armentières and the right flank resting on the village of Maulde, where the frontier cuts across the Escaut River. Within the salient lay the important industrial complexes of Lille and Roubaix. The French 51st Division, which had been placed under Gort's

To British troops in France, it appeared that very little of military importance took place during the eight months of the 'Phoney War'.

command, had already taken up position in the left half of the sector and was covering Tourcoing and Roubaix; leaving the British II Corps (3rd and 4th Divisions) guarding the eastern approaches to Lille whereas I Corps (1st and 2nd Divisions) was deployed in the more open country further to the east. Between the BEF and the enemy was neutral Belgium and in the months that followed the British settled down in the so-called 'Phoney War' to build up its strength in both men and in fortifying the line of the frontier in depth: fortifications that became known as the Gort Line.

In overall command of British and French forces was General Maurice Gamelin, who, like Gort, had excelled during the First World War. Gamelin was a small plump individual whose vision for the defence of France lay very much bound up with the construction of the static Maginot Line, which began in earnest in 1930 along the Franco-German border. Therein lay the Achilles heel of French fortune, as political and financial considerations

Maurice Gamelin commanded French forces until he was sacked on 18 May 1940.

determined it was 'incomplete' in 1939 and the chain of mutually supportive fortifications petered out north of Montmédy. Consequently, when the BEF arrived in France one of their principle tasks – along with the French – was to extend the Maginot Line defences along the border with Belgium to the North Sea. British General Headquarters (GHQ) was opened at Habarcq, some seven miles west of Arras, and it was from there that the progress of the British military build-up in France was directed.

III Corps

By the end of 1939 a third regular division had been formed – the 5th Division – and in January 1940 the first of the Territorial divisions arrived – 48th (South Midland) Division – followed closely by the 50th (Northumbrian) Division and the 51st (Highland) Division. April saw the arrival of the 42nd (East Lancashire) Division and the 44th (Home Counties) Division, giving rise to the formation of III Corps under the command of the very capable Lieutenant General Sir Ronald Adam, an individual already well known to the commander-in-chief. When Gort was appointed CIGS Adam was made Deputy Chief of the Imperial General Staff and when Gort assumed command of the BEF in 1939 he understandably wanted Adam as his Chief of Staff; but in the event Major General Henry Pownall was appointed, a man described as having an 'unruffled imperturbability'.

Sir Ronald Adam commanded III Corps.

The 'Digging' Divisions

By the end of April the BEF had increased its strength to ten divisions, a force that had been augmented by the departure from England of three incomplete Territorial divisions – 12th (Eastern), 23rd (Northumbrian) and 46th (North Midland) – to ease manpower shortages. Neither equipped for a combat role or fully trained, the intention was to use these divisions as pioneers in constructing marshalling yards, airfields and depots. Since there was no question of using such untrained units for fighting, it was stipulated that in each brigade one battalion should undertake training while the other two laboured. When the German attack opened on 10 May these 'digging divisions', which had allowed Hore-Belisha to claim in the House of Commons that Britain had fulfilled her military commitment to France, found themselves unavoidably drawn into the fighting.

Belgian Neutrality

While the Maginot Line was under construction, Belgium was an ally of France, which made the extension of the line along the Franco-Belgian border a political impossibility and one which may even have altered the balance of collaboration between the two countries. Critical to the French was the defence of the industrialised region around Lille, which had been denied to them by the German invasion during the First World War. So when Belgium received a guarantee of their neutrality from Germany in 1937 and attempted to steer a path away from any formal alliance with the French, it became clear in French military and political circles that, in the event of war, if the Germans entered Belgium from the east, their own forces would have to counter such a move from the west.

The French were correct in suspecting a German attack would come through Belgium, a plan confirmed in January 1940 when a German Army major, Helmuth Reinberger, crash-landed in a Messerschmitt Bf 108 near Mechelen-sur-Meuse, instigating the infamous Mechelen Affair. Reinberger was carrying the first plans for the German invasion of Western Europe which, as Gamelin had expected, involved a repeat of the 1914 Schlieffen Plan and a German thrust through Belgium. Although the Belgians were suspicious and suspected deception they eventually concluded that the documents were genuine and even convinced the German government that the plans had been destroyed in the crash and thus remained unseen. At this point it became more and more likely to Belgian military intelligence and Colonel Georges Goethals, the Belgian Military Attaché in Cologne, that the German High Command would not now continue with their original plan. Goethals even went as far as suggesting that a revised plan of attack might draw the Allied armies into north eastern Belgium before the Germans redirected their main thrust further south.

Helmuth Reinberger who crash-landed in a Messerschmitt Bf 108 near Mechelen-sur-Meuse.

Warning the French and British of their concerns, the Belgians at least expected some alteration to Allied strategy. But, despite the evidence to the contrary, Gamelin remained convinced that the main German effort would be between Maastricht and Liège, while Gort and the British Government – still apparently subservient to French military thinking – fell into step behind him by not questioning the wisdom of his decision.

The German plan for invasion

In the circumstances it was hardly surprising that the Germans would rethink their invasion plans. German military planners now took the opportunity to issue a revised plan that not only caught the imagination of Adolf Hitler but reflected the boldness and momentum that came to be associated with *Blitzkrieg*. Alfred Jodl's personal diary records the drastic changes that were made to the German plans after the Mechelen Affair; plans which were masterminded by the 53-year-old *Generalleutnant* Erich von Manstein. While Army Group B under *Generaloberst* Fedor von Bock would continue to attack through north eastern Belgium as the French expected, the main thrust of the German panzer divisions – Army Group A under *Generaloberst* Gerd von Runstedt – would be redirected through the Ardennes to turn north and cut through the British and French lines – exactly as predicted by Georges Goethals. Dubbed 'the Matador's Cloak' by Basil Liddell Hart, Manstein's plan was masterly in its simplicity and adopted the code word *Fall Gelb*.

Erich von Manstein masterminded the final German invasion plan.

Plan D

With Gamelin continuing to ignore any thoughts of a German change of strategy, his first proposal for countering the threat of invasion focussed on the less risky Plan E, which called for Allied forces to advance to the line of the Escaut. Despite this plan being the more sensible, it was discarded in favour of the more easterly River Dyle; Gamelin successfully argued that the anti-tank defences built by the Belgians would allow for a rapid deployment and facilitated the French Seventh Army link-up with the Dutch via Breda.

Thus, the strategic plan – which became known as Plan D – was for French and British forces to cross the border in the event of a German attack and occupy the line of the River Dyle, which runs roughly north and south about thirty miles east of Brussels. The BEF were to deploy between Louvain and Wavre with the French First Army under

Georges Blanchard commanded the French First Army, becoming commander of the French First Army Group in late May 1940.

General Georges Blanchard on the right in the Gembloux Gap and the Belgians who, it was anticipated, would fall back into the gap between the left of the BEF and the right of the General Henri Giraud's Seventh Army.

It was a plan that certainly puzzled many in the BEF who had spent the whole of the previous winter preparing defences behind the Belgian frontier. Now as soon as Germany invaded Belgium all that was to be abandoned and the enemy was to be brought to battle from positions that were unfamiliar and where the defences were already thought to be of a poor quality. If that was not bad enough, there was considerable doubt over the fighting quality of the Belgian forces and their ability to put up a stout resistance.

With the benefit of hindsight there is little doubt that Plan D was a fundamental flaw in the Allied strategy and must certainly be regarded as one of the principle factors in the Fall of France. As early as 13 May, three days after the advance into Belgium had begun, Captain Phillip Gribble, an air liaison officer with the British Air Forces in France HQ was concerned as to why the *Luftwaffe* had been so restrained in their bombing. 'It looks almost as if the Germans want us where we are going. Has the French High command forgotten that the encounter battle is the risk we have always been told to avoid at any cost?'

It was a question that had also been put to Gamelin by his military advisor, Lieutenant Colonel Paul de Villelume, who apparently begged his commander-in-chief to halt the advance while there was still time to do so – a notion that was shared by a number of officers in the BEF. But whatever fears and concerns that may have been apparent in the minds of the advancing British, it was too late; the trap had been sprung and Gamelin's rather lame reply to de Villelume that it was a *fait accompli* was perhaps symptomatic of the air of helplessness that clouded French thinking.

The Dyle Line

Operation David, the code word transmitted to every British Army unit on the Franco-Belgian border, signalled the end of the Phoney War and the move east to the River Dyle. The main fighting force was headed by motorcycle units of the 4/Royal Northumberland Fusiliers and the Morris CS9 Armoured Cars of the 12th Lancers and was carried out, with little interference from enemy activity, by the troop carrying companies of the Royal Army Service Corps (RASC). Gort's plan was to place the 1st and 2nd Divisions on the right flank and the 3rd Division on the left astride Louvain. By way of reserve the 48th (South Midland) Division was ordered to move east of Brussels and the 4th and 50th (Northumbrian)

British infantry advance into Belgium as refugees and Belgian infantry move in the opposite direction.

Divisions to the south. In addition, the 44th (Home Counties) Division was under orders to march to the Escaut south of Oudenaarde and the 42nd (East Lancashire) Division placed on readiness to take up station to their right if needed.

Events on the Meuse
Unbeknown at the time to British commanders was the extent of the German thrust by Army Group A, which had had struck the French Second Army on the Meuse. German advances late on the 13th had hastened a disorganized French retreat, which twenty-four hours later had been reduced to a rout, opening up a dangerous gap. Blanchard had little choice but to order a retirement to avoid being outflanked, which in its turn involved the British I Corps swinging their line back some six miles to the River Lasne to conform to the French retirement. For the I Corps units dug in along the Dyle their initial surprise at being ordered to retire was replaced by the realization that the manoeuvre was to be carried out immediately and under the cover of darkness.

9

Although the Lasne was a poor substitute for the larger Dyle – which in itself was little more than a ditch in places – the BEF was intact and still full of fighting spirit. However, their movements now were dictated by a wider strategic picture that had reduced Gamelin's Plan D to ashes and begun to threaten the whole allied campaign. On 16 May Gort issued his orders for a general withdrawal to the line of the River Senne, having first sent Major General Thomas Eastwood to Caudry to learn of General Gaston Billotte's intentions. Close to retirement when war was declared, the 65-year-old Billotte was commander-in-chief of the French First Army Group and had reportedly burst into tears when informed of the German breakthrough along the Meuse, tears that were shared by a weeping Georges, who announced to his chief of staff that 'our front has been broken at Sedan'. Some historians have argued that the lightning German advance across France was reason enough for his tears; by 16 May armoured columns from Army Group A had advanced so rapidly into French territory that momentarily they lost contact with their headquarters because they had gone beyond field radio range.

Churchill Flies to Paris
The German breakthrough at Sedan was serious enough for Paul Reynaud, the French Prime Minister, to wake Winston Churchill at

Winston Spencer Churchill.

7.30am on 15 May. Churchill listened gravely as Reynaud told him that France was defeated. Adding to the gloom and despondency that now gripped the French senior command was the surrender of Dutch forces after the bombing of Rotterdam – the first occasion in history that aerial bombing had prompted a national surrender. Churchill's decision to fly to Paris with Sir John Dill, who was now Deputy CIGS, came a mere five days after he had formed a national coalition government. In Paris Gamelin told him that German armour had broken through both north and south of Sedan on a fifty mile front and were advancing at incredible speed either towards Amiens and the coast or to Paris itself. Churchill's question as to the whereabouts of the French strategic reserve was met with a shrug from Gamelin – *Aucun*, he replied (there is none). Churchill admits to being taken aback by this rather blunt statement but was left with the distinct impression that there were no answers to be had. But there was to be no rest along the line of the Senne which, for the retreating British units, was only a temporary respite before fresh orders sent them back towards the line of the Escaut. Surely there the Allied armies could consolidate and halt the relentless advance of German forces.

Chapter Two

III Corps on the Escaut

Commanded by Lieutenant General Sir Ronald Adam, the two divisions of III Corps were on the northern flank of the BEF. The 4th Division deployed five battalions forward on a frontage of some five miles, which was a little shorter than the 44th Division, who opted for a defence in depth and occupied the ground on the extreme left flank of the BEF at the junction with the Belgian Army. Centre stage in their sector was the ridge of high ground between Anzegem and Knok.

The 44th Division
On 14 May the 44th Division, under the command of 55-year-old Major General Edmund 'Sigs' Osborne, began arriving on the Escaut. Osborne, a former Royal Engineers officer, was well aware of the critical importance of the high ground which if lost to the enemy would compromise the whole Escaut position. Osborne soon found himself between a rock and a hard place; whatever deployment he decided upon he knew he would face criticism. By placing 132 (Royal West Kent) Brigade on the left flank and 131 (Queen's Royal West Surrey) Brigade on the right – leaving Brigadier Noel Whitty's 133 (Royal Sussex) Brigade in reserve around Waregem – he positioned six of his available battalions along the river. But even with the forward posts on the tow path itself, observation was still limited.

Major General Edmund Osborne commanded the 44th Division.

The first contact with the enemy came not from across the river but from the air at 10.00am on 19 May. Junkers 87s attacked the bridges at Eine and Oudenaarde and the railway station, providing 132 Brigade with

Freepost Plus RTKE-RGRJ-KTTX
Pen & Sword Books Ltd
47 Church Street
BARNSLEY
S70 2AS

DISCOVER MORE ABOUT MILITARY HISTORY

Pen & Sword Books have over 4000 books currently available, our imprints include; Aviation, Naval, Military, Archaeology, Transport, Frontline, Seaforth and the Battleground series, and we cover all periods of history on land, sea and air.

Keep up to date with our new releases by completing and returning the form below (no stamp required if posting in the UK).

Alternatively, if you have access to the internet, please complete your details online via our website at **www.pen-and-sword.co.uk**.

All those subscribing to our mailing list via our website will receive a free e-book, *Mosquito Missions* by Martin W Bowman. Please enter code number ACC1 when subscribing to receive your free e-book.

Mr/Mrs/Ms ....

Address...

Postcode .... Email address..

Website: www.pen-and-sword.co.uk Email: enquiries@pen-and-sword.co.uk
Telephone: 01226 734555   Fax: 01226 734438
Stay in touch: facebook.com/penandswordbooks or follow us on Twitter @penswordbooks

Eyne (bij Audenaerde). — De nieuwe Brug en Scheldezicht

The American Bridge at Eine before it was destroyed in May 1940.

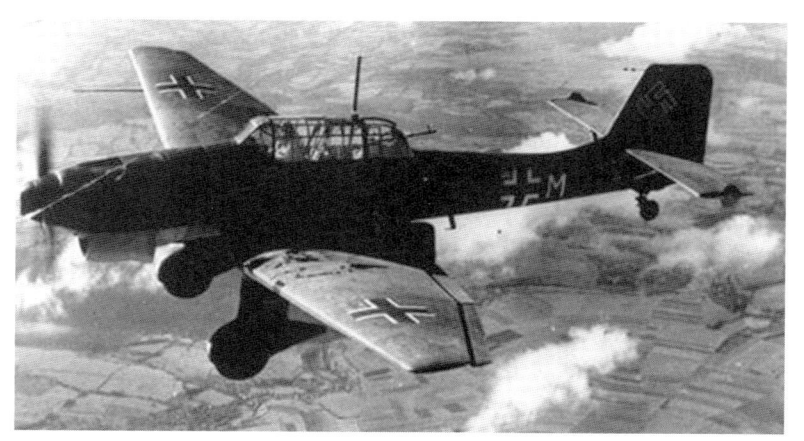

The Junkers 87b Stuka dive bomber provided close air support for German ground troops.

their first battle casualties of the war. Lieutenant Colonel Arthur Chitty, commanding the 4/RWK, recalled thirty bombs being dropped and an ammunition truck parked on the bridge being completely obliterated along with the personnel of an artillery observation post. The other casualties were noted by Captain Stanley Clark to be being mainly from A and B Companies, who were in the forwards posts near the bridges:

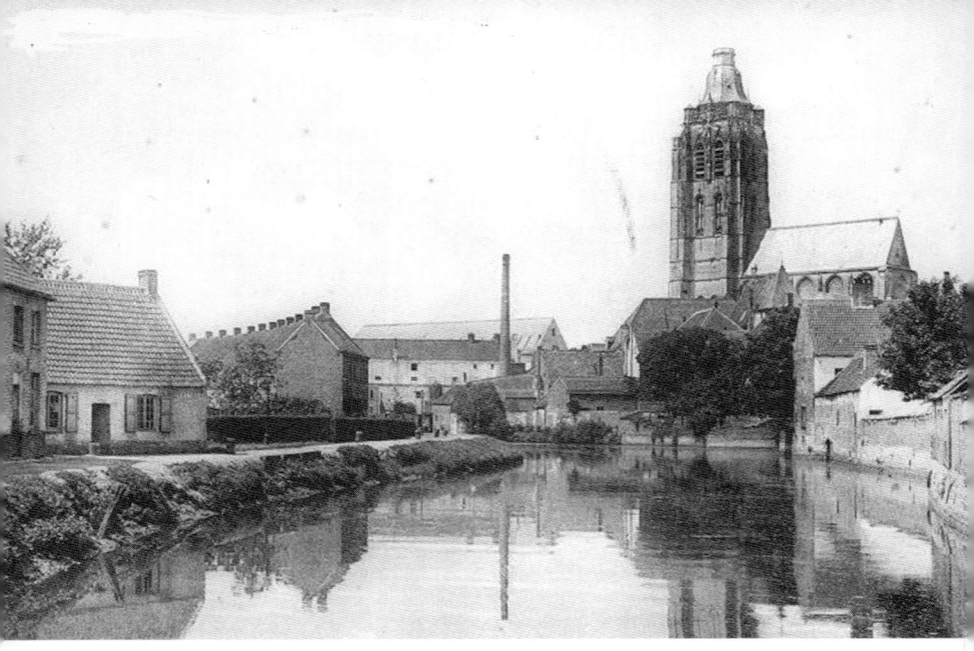

Oudenaarde before the Second World War.

> *It was a nasty shake up and our first taste of war, but there was too much to do to repair the damage done to think then. The Brigade commander ordered the bridges to be blown and by the afternoon there was no contact from the other side ... that evening several shells fell near the town and the first sight was seen of the enemy.*

It was not until the next morning that the first Germans appeared in any real force and were dealt with by a C Company patrol led by Lance Corporal Brookes, who crossed the river and returned with a prisoner. Chitty's men had held the attack but the main German breakthrough came two miles downstream in the 2/Royal East Kent Regiment (2/Buffs) sector.

The Buffs held a frontage of over 2,500 yards and although they were half a mile from the river itself, a drainage canal running in front of their positions was considered enough to stop German armoured vehicles. At 12.30pm the first German units were seen on the hill behind Melden, a presence which developed into artillery fire by late afternoon. An attempted crossing of the river was reported by A Company in the vicinity of the canal loop to the south west. This was the 1/6 Queen's sector and although Captain Richard Rutherford and D Company, who were in position around the Kwaadestraat Château, quickly dealt with this initial incursion, enemy attempts to cross continued into the night. Nevertheless, despite the level of the river dropping some four feet, the advantage was still with the 1/6 Queens who 'dominated the open ground on its front'.

Concerned by the strength of the German incursion, Brigadier John Utterson-Kelso, commanding 131 Brigade, now involved B Company of the 2/Buffs, who were moved across to their right with Captain Francis Crozier in command to support of the 1/6th. This may well have been a mistake, as the Buffs were already under attack from German infantry. Now, under cover of a heavy mortar and artillery bombardment, they crossed the river at the point where the wooded area surrounding Scheldekant Château met the river bank.

Attacking the forward positions of A Company, who were pushed back to the ridge of high ground behind the reserve trenches, the enemy were soon in occupation of the Buff's positions in Huiwede and Petegem,

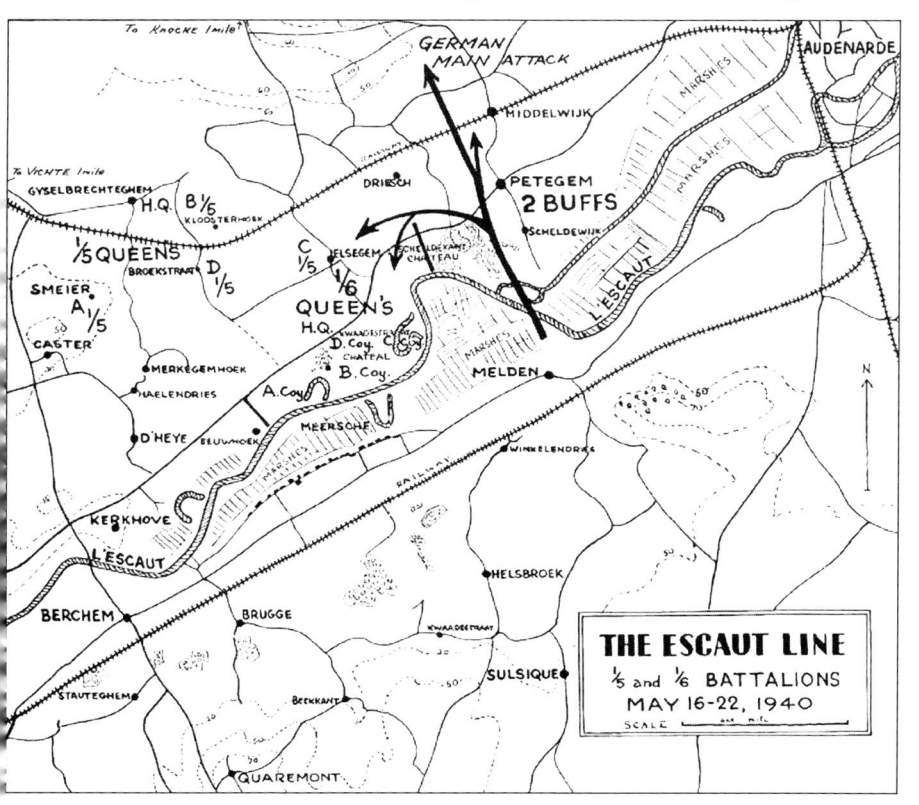

A map depicting the positions of the 1/5 and 1/6 Queens on the Escaut. Taken from *The History of The Queen's Royal Regiment Vol VIII 1924-1948*.

Petegem Railway Station was burnt to the ground, which forced Lieutenant Frazer and his platoon of the 2nd East Kents to new positions further north.

ground which may well have been held had Crozier's B Company not been elsewhere! At Petegem station the burning buildings temporarily forced Lieutenant Frazer's platoon to take up alternative positions to the north in Eekhout. There is certainly evidence of confusion and inexperience hampering operations at this stage. Lieutenant Robert Hodgins, the 131 Brigade Intelligence Officer, wrote that 'no plan was established or received from Division, necessitating continual reference' to the senior staff officer 'for help and guidance'.

Hodgins also felt that the German use of the MP 38 machine pistol in close quarter fighting tactics had taken the British by surprise, a factor that may have adversely impacted on the British troops, who had no little or no experience of automatic small arms fire. That said, the British reply came quickly, beginning at 1.30am on 21 May with a section from the 1/5 Queen's Carrier Platoon who were ordered to clear up isolated pockets of enemy troops. After a somewhat wild and inconclusive exchange with the enemy they returned in time to join Major Lord Edward Sysonby's carrier attack on Petegem from the west. Advancing with two sections through the village, Sysonby found it burning fiercely but, apart from the 'main street being a shambles of dead men and animals' and a section of the 8/Middlesex machine gunners, no Germans were seen until Sysonby's carriers turned left at the crossroads. At this point they came face to face with a column of marching Germans. Opening fire on the enemy with their Bren guns, Sysonby remembers one German firing an anti-tank rifle at him:

> *I shot him in the face with my revolver which was a very fluky shot as we were travelling at about 20mph. We then proceeded on our course for about a mile and a half into the enemy's lines shooting all and sundry we saw.*

The return trip was not without drama. Corporal Arthur Peters was hit and his carrier was knocked out, leaving him with a shattered thigh. Temporarily taken prisoner, he and two others were rescued by Sergeant Reginald Wynn under heavy fire. Wynn was awarded the Distinguished Conduct Medal (DCM) and Sysonby, who was the godson of King George V, received the DSO. Sadly, Peters died of his wounds five days later. Following the carrier attack, two companies of the 1/5 Queen's under Captain Archer did manage to establish themselves east of Petegem, which returned control of the so-called Petegem gap – between themselves and the château at Scheldekant – to the British, who could now bring flanking fire to bear on any attempted enemy advance. But it was a situation that was not to last.

The counter-attack launched by the 1/RWK towards Petegem from Eekhout was initially successful; but hopes of closing the gap were dashed when they were brought to a standstill on the railway line. For a few hours there was stalemate before the German gunners turned their bombardment on the 1/5 Queen's, who were still clinging to ground east of Petegem. Inevitably the hapless defenders were pushed back to new positions behind the railway line and the waiting German infantry flooded through the gap.

Enemy infantry quickly outflanked the Buffs and turned their attentions to the 1/6 Queen's, who rapidly became engaged with an enemy that appeared to have them almost surrounded:

> *The enemy could be seen to be working round the left and rear of B Company. Kwaadestraat Château grounds were badly shelled by guns in the rear, presumably our own, and small parties of enemy penetrated the grounds, but were driven out by a counter-attack by members of Battalion Headquarters. The recaptured posts were occupied by C Company, 1/5 Queen's, which had just arrived as a reinforcement. About 8.00pm the Germans reached Elsegem and were firing into the flank and rear of the Kwaadestraat Château grounds. At the same time news arrived*

Elsegem Château was once a magnificent building.

> that the enemy was also across the Escaut on the right of the 1/6 Queen's front, and this appeared to be confirmed by a display of white Very lights to the north and west of Eeekhoet ... Firing was now continuous; several fresh parties of the enemy had again got a foothold in the Château grounds and no more reserves were left to deal with them, so at 9.15pm Lieut-Colonel Hughes decided to extricate the remainder of the battalion before the position was completely surrounded.

As night fell the remnants of 131 Brigade fought their way back over the railway line, where they met the 2/Royal Sussex who had been brought forward to fill the gap. 131 Brigade reformed north of Courtrai late on 22 May, where the 1/5th numbered twenty-two officers and 447 other ranks while the 1/6th were reorganised into three companies. Of the reported 400 other rank casualties in the 1/6th over 130 were taken prisoner but, like their sister battalion, the number of wounded remained imprecise. Amongst those captured was Sergeant Alex Horwood who was serving with B Company, 1/6 Queens. Horwood's escape from captivity and subsequent evacuation from Dunkirk was blazoned over the front pages of the popular press and

Sergeant Alec Horwood.

resulted in the award of the DCM. He would later go on to be awarded the VC in 1944.

Meanwhile at Oudenaarde the enemy incursions on the 2/Buff's front had put pressure on the 4/RWK headquarters at Moregem Château and, although well defended by Major Marcus Keane, two companies were overrun before the order to withdraw was given. Keane, along with two companies of 5/RWK, had been ordered to cover the flank of the battalion as it broke contact with the enemy. Sergeant Frank Jezard, the MT Transport Sergeant, was at the château on 22 May when the orders to withdraw were relayed to all ranks:

> *First of all we loaded all the casualties into a carrier ... having got them safely on board PSM* [Platoon Sergeant Major] *Chapman said, 'Well boys here we go,' and we made our way to the main gate. We reached the gate and decided the best way out would be round the back and through the grounds and fields. We had not gone far when someone asked, 'who can drive a truck?' Everyone looked round and then I saw a 15cwt* [truck] *beneath a tree. It had been plastered all day along one side with shrapnel – one rear tyre had been ripped open but this didn't worry us.*

Moregem Château as the 4th Royal West Kents would have seen it in May 1940.

Jezard's account of the fighting around the château differs slightly from that of Lieutenant Colonel Chitty, who reported that 'the men fought to the end and twenty signallers, the officer's mess cooks and drivers were among the casualties'. Clearly some managed to escape as Jezard says there were twenty men in his party, including Sergeant Humphrey, the Cook Sergeant, and PSM Arthur Chapman, commanding 5 Platoon, who was later singled out for the award of the DCM. Whether some fought on to the end is uncertain but we do know Marcus Keane was killed while commanding the rearguard. It is worth noting that the 5/RWK war diary reported isolated groups of enemy establishing themselves in Oudenaarde on 21 May, having crossed at the junction between them and the 4/RWK.

The 4th Division

Commanding the division was Major General Dudley Johnson, who was already the recipient of the DSO and bar and the MC when he was awarded the VC whilst in command of the 2/Royal Sussex in November 1918. Appointed to command the division in 1938, he was responsible for a six mile sector of the Escaut on the right of the 44th Division, a sector that included the Kerkhove bridge. Dug in around the bridge was A Company of the 1/East Surrey Regiment, who occupied the village and were in touch with B Company on the left along the river bank. Across the river at Berchem, C and D Companies with the battalion's carriers were tasked with preventing enemy patrols from reaching the bridge. Overlooking the Surrey's position was Mont de l'Enclus, a high point

Major General Dudley Johnson commanded the 4th Division.

The high ground of Mont de l'Enclus overlooked the Surrey's positions.

from which enemy artillery observers had an uninterrupted view. 'It gave the German gunners,' wrote Lieutenant Colonel Reginald Boxshall, 'good observation, and we were heavily and accurately shelled.'

Working alongside 11 Brigade were the sappers of 7/Field Company who, in addition to preparing the bridge at Kerkhove for demolition, were also fortifying the riverside buildings. Second Lieutenant Curtis was at the bridge:

> Road blocks had been erected east of the bridge and a light screen of the Surreys were ready to hold back the Germans if they appeared. Assault boats were issued to the Surreys so they could return across the river after the bridge was blown. Shortly after 23.00 hours [10.00pm] on May 19, the Adjutant of 3 Div rearguard arrived to say the rear-most battalion was some miles away, and that the bridge should not be blown until it had crossed. It was now a question of waiting to see who would arrive first, 3 Div or the enemy.

Lieutenant Colonel Boxshall has no doubt that it was *his* orders that delayed the blowing of the bridge and writes that it was a battalion of Sherwood Foresters that were the last to cross the river before the order was given for its destruction. At what point Boxshall brought C and D Companies back is not clear but 'eventually', he wrote,' the Germans occupied all the east bank of the River Escaut'.

The battle at the bridge continued for most of the day as the Germans tried to cross the river under a curtain of heavy shellfire. The Regimental Aid Post received a direct hit, killing or wounding everyone who was working there, though fortunately Lieutenant Donald Bird, the battalion medical officer, was dealing with casualties elsewhere at the time. Sadly, the 26-year-old Bird was not to return home and died in June 1940 at Malo-les-Bains. Boxshall noted with some alarm that all the battalion's anti-tank guns were also knocked out during this bombardment. On the Surrey's right flank, the 2/Lancashire Fusiliers were also under a heavy artillery and mortar bombardment. Major Lawrence Manly, noting the accuracy was remarkable, added, 'Battalion Headquarters, A Company and B Company suffered the most'. Yet, despite the profusion of shellfire, the East Surreys and Lancashire Fusiliers were managing to hold their own, a state of affairs that was not replicated on the left flank, as Lieutenant Colonel Bill Green's 5/Northamptons came under increasing pressure.

The 41-year-old Green was a decorated Royal Flying Corps (RFC) flying ace in the First World War and credited with nine victories between

A sapper from 211 Field Park Company (44th Division) preparing to demolish a section of railway line by using Mototov Cocktails.

January and September 1918. Transferring to the Northamptonshire Regiment in 1921, he assumed command of the battalion in 1938. Now, with D Company in touch with the Queen's on the left, the battalion was strung out along two thousand yards of the Escaut. Although Boxshall makes no mention of this in his account, A Company of the Northamptons, under the command of Captain Hart, were dug in along the eastern edge of Berchem and it was there that the battalion had their first contact with the enemy:

> *A Company were well hidden in scattered houses on the edge of the village ... At about 11.00am a group of about twelve apparent refugees approached. To Captain Hart it seemed that they were walking with a somewhat martial stride and his suspicions were confirmed when they were followed by about twenty cyclists, riding in pairs, and a lorry. The section covering the road held their fire until the cyclists were a good target at close range and opened fire with Bren and rifles.'*

The first burst of fire took down the majority of the cyclists, prompting the marching 'refugees' to break for cover and return fire. As the attack became more determined the company were withdrawn across the river by boat, courtesy of 7/Field Company. Hart was given an immediate award of the MC and Privates Sharpe and Herbert the Military Medal (MM).

The bombardment that was causing havoc at Kerkhove was also being directed at the Northamptons and after some very fierce fighting the Germans managed to establish themselves in a small orchard on D Company's front and, although they were discouraged from widening their foothold by a Northamptonshire bayonet charge, D Company sustained heavy casualties, reducing their effective strength to less than two platoons. Brought into the fight as support, C Company lost around a third of their strength before the battalion front was readjusted and it was only the arrival of the 6/Black Watch during the night that prevented the enemy from working found the flank and surrounding the battalion.

Early on 22 May patrols from A Company established the Germans were now across the river in some strength and it was not long before they directed their attentions towards Captain John Johnson's C Company positions. After Johnson was killed by a direct hit, the company – by now very much reduced in numbers – got away only after Green ordered up the carrier platoon to hold the enemy, an order that resulted in five of the carriers being destroyed and eleven of its twenty-eight men being killed.

Where the Royal Artillery were able to establish effective forward observation, their 25-pounder gun crews were very successful in breaking up German troop movements across the Escaut.

Surrounded and out of ammunition, the remaining men of the carrier platoon fought their way clear with grenades. The orders to withdraw came not a moment too soon. The battalion had suffered enormously and, with eleven officers killed or wounded and C Company less than forty strong, the remaining rifle companies could only muster some sixty-five men apiece. Worse still was the news that Lieutenant Colonel Green had been killed at Teigem.

Back on the 1/East Surrey's front at Kerkhove, the Germans had also got across the river and, with the battalion's left flank turned, it looked very much as if the situation was fast becoming untenable; a situation that did not prevent Captain Ricketts from leading a counter-attack with C Company:

> *It all started with a sergeant arriving at my position very much out of breath and with a revolver in his hand to tell me A Company were surrounded and they needed the reserve company to get them out ... I went in deployed in Y formation. The only opposition met on our way came from a house and a party of apparent Fifth Columnists which we despatched, with me on the Bren and PSM Bob Gibson bowling a couple of Mills bombs. I eventually arrived at A Company's position and found Captain Finch White who told me he was intact, but was receiving a belting and could do with some help.*

Ricketts was wounded along with Second Lieutenant Meredith in the attack, which, in the event, turned out not to be needed – it was later in the day that A Company would have appreciated Rickett's assistance! Shortly after the C Company counter-attack the Brigade Major arrived at Battalion Headquarters with orders to withdraw immediately. Boxshall recalled that he was unhappy with the order:

> *As it meant moving men over open ground exposed to full view from enemy observation points. However, as both flank battalions were on the move I had no choice. I issued orders by runner (all lines had been cut), and backed them up with liaison officers in carriers. Three companies got the orders, but A Company on the right did not.*

Pinned down by enemy fire and finding themselves isolated and outflanked, Captain Finch White realised that the Germans were now across the river on both flanks and waited until dark to find out for himself what was taking place:

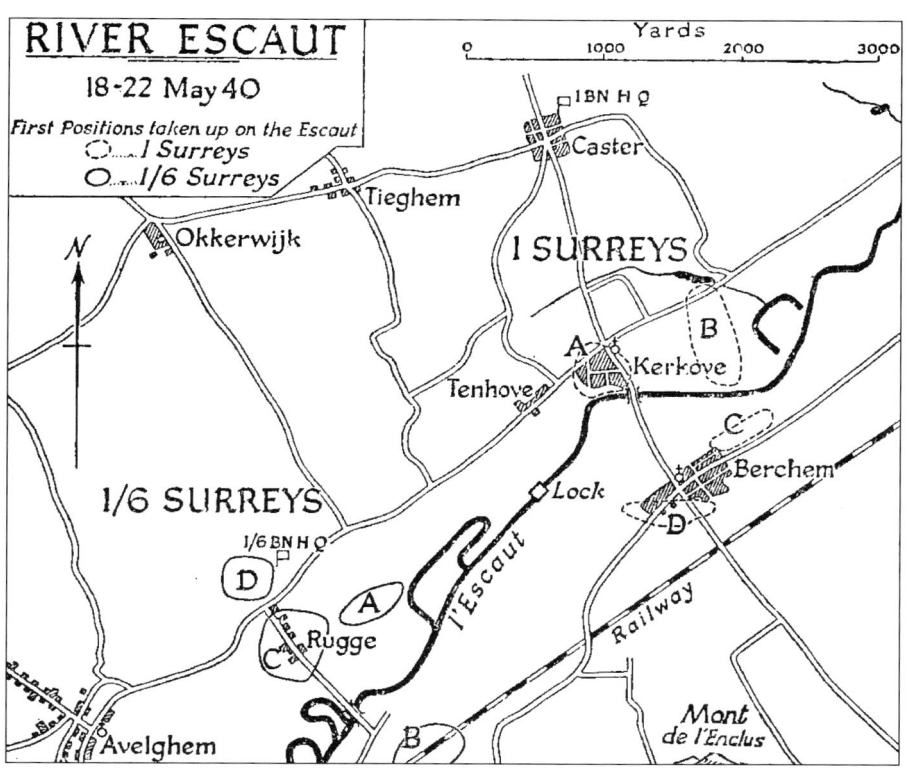

A map of the East Surrey deployment on the Escaut taken from the *History of the East Surrey Regiment Vol IV.*

> After going a short distance I was fired upon from what had been the position of Battalion Headquarters and it was clear we had to get out quickly ...We withdrew with the Germans advancing parallel to us on each flank. Fortunately they took no notice of us. We did come under heavy machine gun fire from our own rearguard, not the Surreys, and had to take cover ... We then got a lift in some transport and rejoined the battalion.'

The Surrey's withdrawal was not without cost. Machine gunned by low flying aircraft as they retired from the Escaut valley, Boxshall's carrier was hit by anti-tank tracer that penetrated the vehicle, badly bruising him and wounding his second in command, Major Ken Lawton.

It was a similar story on the 2/Lancashire Fusilier's front. At 3.00pm on 22 May news that the right flank had given way prompted Lieutenant

Colonel Leslie Rougier to bring into play the carrier platoon under the command of Captain Hugh Woollatt to form a defensive flank. Last seen at B Company Headquarters, Woollatt was taken prisoner shortly before the orders to retire to the Gort line were received, a move that cost the 44-year-old Rougier his life when he was killed by shellfire near the railway cutting south of the Tiegem Ridge. Command was assumed by Lawrence Manly, who brought the battalion out of action with over 175 officers and men either killed, wounded or missing.

The 2/Duke of Cornwall's Light Infantry (DCLI), under the command of Lieutenant Colonel Eric Rushton, arrived on the Escaut just before midnight on 18 May. With a frontage of just over a mile to defend, the battalion linked up with the 2/Beds and Herts on their right and the 2/Lancashire Fusiliers on their left. There were two bridges in the Cornishmen's sector, one east of Meerstraat, which had been demolished, and the road bridge at Rugge which was still intact. About half a mile north-west of the river was a water course called the Rijtgracht that ran parallel to the river, while to the east was the high ground of Mont de l'Enclus, which overlooked the whole of the divisional sector. Rushton was immediately faced with a distinctly unenviable sector to defend. With the ground between the river and the Rijtgracht practically impossible to defend, after consultation with Brigadier Barker he finally withdrew the bulk of his battalion behind the Rijtgracht, leaving only section posts along the river bank. The battalion historian remarking that:

No other cover existed in the flat water-meadows, intersected by ditches, apart from the ditches themselves and the willows growing along them, which were obvious ranging marks for enemy weapons.

These new positions were dug overnight on 20 May with assistance from a company of the 1/6 East Surreys, who were being held in reserve.

The morning of 21 May saw the German assault on the Escaut begin in earnest; but the battalion successfully held a determined German attempt to cross the river to the accompaniment of an enemy artillery bombardment that many, who had survived the First World War, claimed was heavier than they had previously experienced. The war diary records the enemy bombardment was some six hours in duration, during which the village of Rugge was very badly damaged. Captain Edwin Pentreath, commanding A Company, recalled one of his signallers completely disregarding the rain of high explosive:

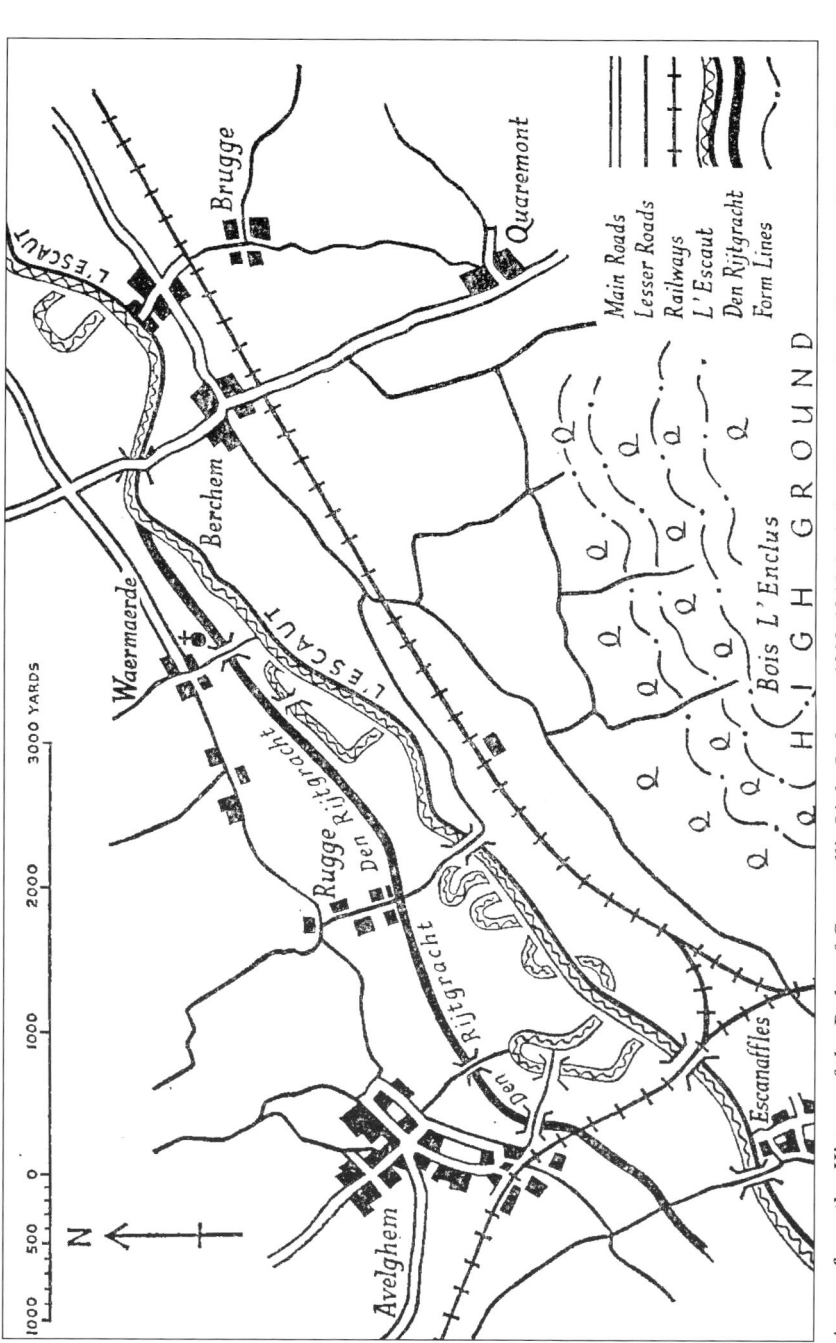

A map from the *History of the Duke of Cornwall's Light Infantry 1939-1945* depicting the sector from Brugge to Escanaffles and showing the location of the Rijgracht.

> *In this inferno I came upon a young Cockney, Signaller Palmer, in full view of the enemy, repairing the line between C Coy and A Coy, hatless, unconcerned, whistling merrily. Whereas I was falling flat on my face in honour of each close shell burst, Palmer was simply ignoring them. When I remonstrated with him he said 'The so-and-so's are giving me so much repairing to do that if I stopped for each shell I'd never keep up with them.*

At 10.05pm A and B Companies were heavily attacked and, despite the weight of fire being brought down on them, German infantry were reportedly in possession of the bridge. It was essential to discover the exact nature of this incursion and, to that end, Captain Pentreath with Privates Clarke and Cox, managed to cover the 600 yards of open ground to the river bank unobserved. The three men were about 500 yards from the bridge where Cox was left on the bank and Pentreath and Clarke then crawled and swam to within sight of the bridge where Pentreath managed to make a sketch of the enemy dispositions. Briefly showing himself, the subsequent volley of enemy fire was fortunately not accurate and appeared to be directed from the opposite bank. All three men returned safely with the information that the bridge was, at the time of Pentreath's observations, unoccupied. Pentreath's MC and Clarke's MM were announced in June 1940. At 3.30am on 22 May the battalion was relieved by the 1/6 East Surreys. Apart from their dead, several wounded men had to be left behind in the care of the relieving battalion. Sadly, Rushton was killed on the Dunkirk beaches on 1 June and is commemorated on the Dunkirk Memorial.

At Avelgem Lieutenant Colonel James Birch, commanding the 2/Bedfordshire and Hertfordshires, had established his headquarters in a small café close to the main cross roads. Deploying C Company at Escanaffles on the eastern bank of the river with orders that the bridge was not to fall into enemy hands, the remaining companies – presumably under orders from Brigadier Evelyn Barker, commanding 10 Brigade – were directed to positions on the forward edge of Mont de l'Enclus. In his account Birch writes that he met Barker and Major General Johnston on Mont de l'Enclus and was immediately told to move his men to the east and south faces of the hill, leaving him

Brigadier Evelyn Barker.

28

The demolished bridge at Escanaffles where 'bits and pieces of the bridge were thrown high in the sky'.

to wonder just how he was going to hold the position with so few men. However, sanity appears to have prevailed as the orders were changed yet again, resulting in the battalion taking up new positions, this time on the western bank of the river. Nevertheless there was still a sticky moment or two before C Company were finally brought back across the bridge:

> *Eventually the last section under the command of Lance Corporal Major came doubling back over the bridge followed at a distance by the head of a column of refugees. The sapper sergeant called upon the civilians to go back but they paid no heed. He then told the troops to run flat out and he would press the plunger in a minute. Lance Corporal Major and his section then completed an Olympic 100 metre dash when there was a deafening roar as one and a half tons of explosive charge erupted and bits and pieces of the bridge were thrown high in the sky.*

Birch's account is quite critical of the 'marching and counter-marching' his battalion had been subjected to on 19 May, writing that, 'I have no doubt that there was good reason for it, but I did regret that I had no opportunity of making a good recce of the canal bank on such a vast front before the enemy arrived'. Birch neglects to mention that the flat and featureless ground between the river and Avelgem gave his forward platoons little cover from enemy artillery and mortar attack.

As they had done further north, German troops made their first appearance on the far bank on the morning of 20 May. Birch's unease at the extent to which the battalion's positions were overlooked was not improved by the first casualties at the hands of enemy snipers lodged in the industrial buildings at Escanaffles. At 11.00am 12 Platoon were subjected to a heavy mortar attack, during which PSM Warren was badly wounded, which only served to add to Birch's overall apprehension as to the vulnerability of his canal side defences. Like Lieutenant Colonel Rushton and the DCLI, he was between a rock and a hard place. If he remained where he was the battalion would continue to take heavy casualties but if he withdrew to a safer line German infantry would be given the opportunity of crossing the river and establishing themselves on the western bank:

The very exposed positions on the edge of the canal could not be held and I was much concerned. I moved some carriers to increase the fire power in this area and that night fresh positions were dug. I had made a thorough reconnaissance of our side of the 'billiard table' and with the Brigadier decided to make our main defence along the courant [the Rijtgracht] *about 1000 yards back from the canal with the forward platoons still close to the canal.*

All troops were in their new positions by dawn on 21 May and it was not long before German troops – as expected – began filtering over the blown bridge.

The British reply was a counter-attack launched by one platoon of C Company supported by artillery. The plan involved Second Lieutenant David Muirhead and 15 Platoon approaching the enemy from a flank and, with support from 13 Platoon and guns of 22/Field Regiment, check the German incursion. Second Lieutenant Robin Medley witnessed the attack:

The guns fired bang on time and the ground around the target area erupted with explosions, but as yet the attacking troops could not be seen as they were hidden from view. After some eight minutes the attacking platoon came into view with the soldiers advancing steadily, rifles and bayonets across their chests ... it was a splendid sight and, as far as could be seen there were no gaps in the lines. Meanwhile, the artillery was pounding the objective and 13 Platoon was firing onto the enemy bank of the canal with their Brens. Bang on time the assault charged as the guns lifted ... giving 15 Platoon time to deploy and firm up its objective. After sixteen minutes the guns stopped firing and there was a sudden silence.

Birch is more matter-of-fact than Medley in his account and simply tells us that the enemy 'cleared off when they saw the attack was on'; but Muirhead's counter-attack clearly had the desired effect and the battalion was not bothered by infantry attack again during its short occupation of the river. The orders to withdraw arrive later that night and, with the carrier platoon forming the rearguard, the Beds and Herts began their move west at 9.00pm under cover of darkness.

Chapter Three

II Corps on the Escaut

Commanded by Lieutenant General Alan Brooke, II Corps were in the centre of the British line and to some extent benefitted from the calibre of their senior commanders. It is interesting to observe that Brooke, Alexander and Montgomery all deployed the highest concentration of firepower along the river line. The 3rd Division did not arrive until the afternoon of 19 May and the 1st Division even later, arriving in the early evening and in an almost totally exhausted state.

The 3rd Division
The 3rd Division frontage on the Escaut involved all three brigades, with 7 (Guards) Brigade sandwiched between 9 Brigade on the left and 8 Brigade on the right. Brigadier Jack Whitaker and 7 (Guards) Brigade moved into position on 19 May, covering a sector one mile east of Helkijn to the junction of the Escaut and the Canal de l'Espierres. Whitaker's deployment saw the 2/Grenadier Guards on the left and centred on Helkijn itself and the 1/Grenadier Guards on the right, with their HQ at Château d'Espierres. Lieutenant Colonel John Lloyd, commanding the

The 1st Battalion Grenadier guards established their HQ in the magnificent Château d'Espierres.

battalion, had already received orders to hold the road bridge at Helkijn and form a bridgehead on the eastern side of the river to await the arrival of 8 Brigade. There were some tense hours before the missing brigade crossed the river and relieved the 1/Coldstream that had been slotted into the line in place of Brigadier Christopher Woolner's 8 Brigade. The bridge was finally blown at 2.00am on 20 May.

All along the 7 Brigade frontage the river ran through a wide expanse of marshy ground devoid of natural camouflage and 'unapproachable in daylight except by ditch crawling'. With the bridges blown and the dam situated opposite the 1/Grenadier's sector plugged with barbed wire, they sat waiting for the Germans to arrive on the opposite bank. It was not long before they put in an appearance. At 6.30am on 20 May, Major Rupert Colvin (2/Grenadiers) caught sight of several enemy soldiers

The 1st Battalion Grenadier Guard's sector ran from the Sucrerie at Helkijn to the junction of the Escaut and the Canal d'Espierres.

crawling back from the eastern edge of the river. Half an hour later the enemy opened up with a heavy artillery bombardment and Colvin gave orders for HQ Company to be ready to make an immediate counter-attack on the bridge as the section holding it was already under severe machine gun fire and in difficulties. As the artillery attack continued in its ferocity it was joined by salvos of fire from 4-inch mortars. Colvin's concern about his left flank – where a gap existed between No.1 Company and the right flank of 9 Brigade – became a reality at 11.30am when the enemy assault focussed on this very sector.

The reports of columns of German infantry seen debussing some 800 yards from the river served only to underline the strength of enemy forces and their determination to cross the river. It was, wrote Rupert Colvin, 'a pretty tense couple of hours but repeated attempts by the enemy to cross the canal failed'. Fortunately, with the addition of the Coldstream Carrier and Mortar Platoons, the position was more or less stabilised by 2.00pm and apart from sniping and occasion bursts of machine gun fire there was no more enemy activity that day. On 22 May orders were received for the brigade to withdraw, along with the remainder of the 3rd Division.

The 1st Division

Much of the divisional sector was overlooked by the prominence of Mont St Aubert on the eastern side of the river, a feature that had not gone unnoticed by Lieutenant Colonel Lionel Bootle-Wilbraham, commanding the 2/Coldstream Guards at Pecq. When he arrived on the Escaut in the early afternoon of 19 May the sappers were already preparing the road bridge for demolition. Deploying Nos.1 and 3 Companies along the river, he kept No.2 Company in reserve and covered the roads leading into the village with No.4 Company who were later moved into the tannery in the

The tannery at Pecq where No.4 Company of the 2nd Coldstream were based.

The 2ⁿᵈ Battalion Hampshires shared the Château de Bourgogne with Beckwith-Smith and 1 (Guards) Brigade.

north of the village. Brigadier Merton Beckwith-Smith had placed the 2/Hampshires in reserve a mile to the west at Estaimbourg along with 1 Brigade HQ at Château du Bourgogne. To the right of the Coldstream were the 3/Grenadiers, who had the 2/North Staffordshires on their right flank.

Lieutenant Jimmy Langley, who was serving with the Coldstream No.3 Company, was placed in command of the Pecq bridge by his company commander, Major Angus McCorquodale. With him was Sergeant Smith, a signaller from HQ Company, who manned the field telephone, and an RE Officer whose job it was to blow the bridge on Langley's command. Langley writes he was more than a little alarmed at McCorquodale's orders for Sergeant Smith to shoot him if he sat or lay down:

Brigadier Merton Beckwith-Smith.

The implications of this order may not have been immediately clear to Sergeant Smith who looked somewhat startled, but they were to me and I began to protest.

'Shut up Jimmy. Surely you realize that the moment you sit or lie down you will go to sleep and that you are not going to do. Repeat my order, Sergeant Smith.'

'The moment Mr Langley tried to sit or lie down I am to shoot him.'

Right, if I find Mr. Langley alive and asleep you will know what to expect. Good luck!

Langley was so alarmed by this that he later wrote he did not even dare go near the sides of the bridge in case Sergeant Smith should consider he was leaning against the bridge and thus about to sit down. At 1.00am a very relieved Langley gave the order for the bridge to be blown and joined his platoon by the river bank.

Apart from the blowing of the Pecq bridge on 20 May there was very little enemy activity to interfere with the Coldstream's preparations for the arrival of the German 31st Infantry Division. The first contact came on the No.1 Company front with the death of Captain Evelyn Boscawen, who was sniped during the night from the opposite bank by German forces who were clearly gathering for a major attack the following

Lieutenant Jimmy Langley.

morning. It came shortly before dawn with a violent and sudden assault – which undoubtedly was being directed by observation from Mont St

The Bridge at Pecq as it was in May 1940.

Aubert – and succeeded in establishing a bridgehead at the boundary between the two Guards' battalions.

The first Bootle-Wilbraham heard of the enemy incursion was at around midday. After a rapid reorganization of the defences around Battalion Headquarters at the Château on the N510 Lille road, Captain Charles Fane was ordered to take his carriers up to the rising ground on the right of No.1 Company to form a defensive flank. He was killed shortly afterwards by shellfire:

Captain Evelyn Boscawen.

In the meantime a gun had opened fire to our right rear and shells from it were landing 150 yards north of Battalion Headquarters. I could not help wondering whether the Germans had not succeeded in getting an infantry gun across the river and were working their way up between the Grenadiers and ourselves to Estaimbourg. Bunty Stewart-Brown went forward to take command of 1 and 2 Companies and the carrier platoon. Sometime later he reported the Pecq – Pont-a-Chin road was held and there did not appear to be any enemy between the road and the canal ... For five minutes the road to the Château was searched by a battery of medium guns. There was one direct hit amongst

The Château du Biez may well have been the 'unamed château on the road to Lille' referred to by Lieutenant Colonel Bootle-Wilbraham.

The barn that housed the 3rd Battalion Grenadier Guards' No.4 Company is now a private house.

> *pioneers and a number of men were killed and wounded, the latter including CQMS Burnett. One of the signallers, a very young boy, burst into tears, not so much from fright as because two of his pals had been killed and he was splattered with their blood. That was the climax of the battle. From then on things improved.*

Meanwhile on the Grenadiers' front, Guardsman Les Drinkwater, serving with No. 4 Company, was in a large barn that was screened from enemy observation by the river side vegetation. Drinkwater's company was at the critical junction of the two Guards' battalions, a position which was giving Major Reggie Alston-Roberts-West, commanding the company, some anxious moments. Sending Drinkwater and Sergeant Bullock – presumably to report on the situation on the left flank – the two men found themselves in the thick of the fighting, with enemy infantry from IR 12 forming the German spearhead and establishing themselves in the wood on the ridge of high ground known today as Poplar Ridge:

> *When we arrived we realised the enemy was determined to wipe out this flank. We were lying down behind a bush, bullets were cracking over our bodies, trench mortar bombs and shrapnel shells were exploding. The din was terrible. To our amazement,*

through all this noise, we could hear the familiar sound of a Bren gun firing as if it was defying the whole German Army.

It may not have been the whole German army but if *Hauptmann* Lothar Ambrosius – commanding the IR 12 assault – is correct in his account, they were inflicting a considerable number of casualties on the enemy infantry attempting to cross the river. Drinkwater writes that his admiration for the two men firing the Bren gun was shattered by a direct hit, which blew Guardsman Arthur Rice 'clean through the bush' and badly wounded Guardsman George Button who was firing the Bren. Dragging a blinded Button by the hand and shouting for Drinkwater to follow him, Bullock was last seen 'running like blazes'. Despite Rice pleading to be left, Drinkwater remained with the badly wounded guardsman, convinced that he would soon become a prisoner. But fortune was smiling that day and they both eventually arrived back at the barn, where Rice was loaded onto one of the two company trucks:

Hauptmann Lothar Ambrosius.

> *We were very fortunate, the large double doors faced the bank – the enemy were closing in from the rear. A decision had been made for the first truck to turn left, the other right. On clearing the barn we ran straight into the enemy – the essence of surprise was with us. At this stage the enemy dared not fire in case they hit each other; we were through, a hail of bullets hit our truck, wounding the driver, but we continued and were soon over a ridge of high ground and out of sight of the enemy.*

Les Drinkwater may have escaped captivity but the seriousness of the German advance was still threatening the left flank, giving Major Allan Adair little choice but to counter-attack with his reserve company. At 11.30am No.3 Company, with Captain Lewis Starkey in command, supported by three carriers led by Lieutenant Heber Reynall-Pack, advanced towards the German positions now established at the base of Poplar Ridge. 'It was', wrote Allan Adair, 'a

Major Allan Adair commanded the 3rd Battalion Grenadier Guards.

magnificent and inspiring sight to see the company dash forward through the cornfield and vanish out of sight over the ridge'. Suicidal was the word that immediately sprang to Guardsman Bill Lewcock's mind as he and his comrades advanced across the cornfield in open formation. Met with a hail of machine gun fire, No.3 Company was soon taking significant casualties, which included Captain Robert Abell-Smith, the second-in-command of the company. Lewcock saw Lieutenant the Duke of Northumberland go down at the head of his platoon and recalled that the attack was in great danger of stalling in the face of mounting casualties:

Lieutenant the Duke of Northumberland.

At this stage the attack would probably not have been successful had it not been for the action of two individual Grenadiers. The first was Lieutenant Reynall-Pack, in command of the carrier platoon, who took his carriers across the bullet-swept ground, using them as though they were tanks, and silenced the machine guns on the left by hurling grenades into the midst of the crews: he was killed in his carrier immediately afterwards. The second was L/Cpl [Harry] Nicholls.

Harry Nicholls was on the left of the No. 3 Company advance. Despite already being wounded in the arm by shrapnel, he seized the initiative as the company became bogged down with casualties. Running forward with a Bren gun and firing from the hip, he silenced three enemy machine gun posts, during which time he was again wounded in the head. Moving forward he continued to bring fire to bear on the enemy until his ammunition ran out.

Guardsman Percy Nash was with Nicholls as he dashed forward; he remembered feeding Nicholls with ammunition for the Bren gun as they advanced

Lance Corporal Harry Nicholls VC.

in short rushes towards the enemy. After silencing the machine gun posts at Poplar Ridge, Nash says Nicholls then began firing on the enemy who were crossing the river and sank at least two boats before their ammunition ran out. Nash was mentioned in despatches and promoted to sergeant while Nicholls – on Nash's evidence – was reported as missing believed killed and his 'posthumous' VC was subsequently received by

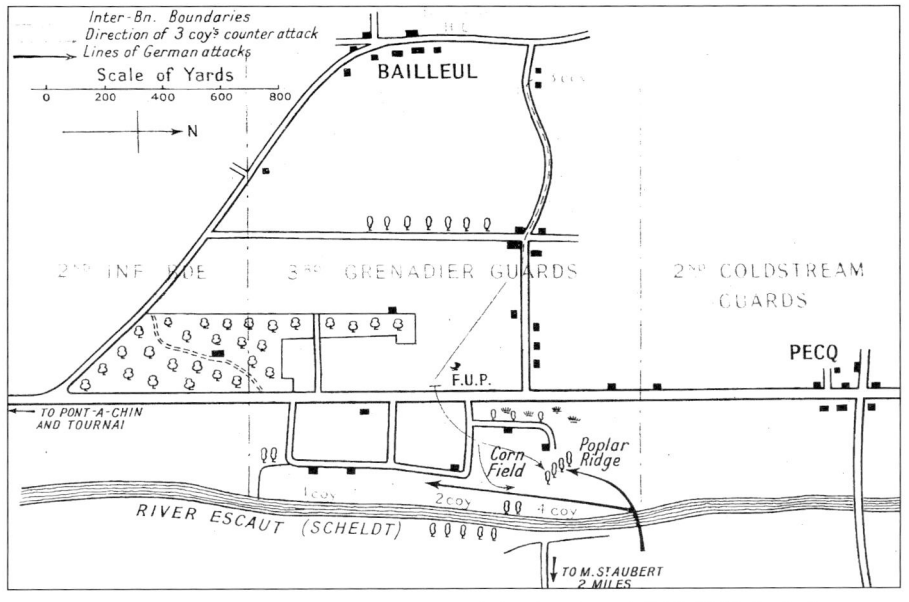

A map taken from *The Grenadier Guards in the War of 1939-1945* depicting the positions of the Grenadier and Coldstream Guards around Pecq.

An artist's impression of Harry Nicholls on Poplar Ridge.

his wife Connie. It was only after the presentation at Buckingham Palace that it was learnt Nicholls was a prisoner and in hospital in Germany and he was finally presented with his cross at Buckingham Palace in June 1945.

But it was not entirely a Guards' affair. The counter attack was supported by A Company of the 2/North Staffordshires under the command of 41-year-old Major Frederick Matthews, who was ordered to attack with two platoons and the battalion's carriers from Esquelmes – a plan which failed to manifest itself fully but did in the event prevent any potential enemy advance penetrating beyond the main N50 road. Sadly, Matthews was killed during the attack and, although his body was not recovered at the time, he was later found during the battlefield clear-up. Sending a carrier back to look for any trace of Major Matthews, a seriously wounded Captain Birch and a corporal of the 3/Grenadiers were

The Bren gun was the primary British and Commonwealth forces light machine gun during the Second World War.

The Universal Carrier was more commonly known as the Bren Gun Carrier. This photograph was taken during an exercise in France prior to May 1940.

found by the shrine close to the N50. Birch later recounted how he and the Grenadier corporal had actually been taken prisoner but the Germans had left them to fetch two stretchers. In the short space of time that elapsed Corporal Wade arrived and just managed to get the two wounded men on the carrier before the Germans returned. Both men were successfully evacuated to England.

The counter-attack – which had accounted for some sixty Germans killed and over 130 wounded – forced the IR 12 bridgehead from the west bank of the river and restored some resemblance of calm to the battlefield. Understandably the greater number of casualties suffered in the fighting were in the ranks of the 3/Grenadier Guards, where twenty men were taken prisoner and six officers and some fifty-one other ranks were either killed in action, missing or died of wounds, including Drinkwater's company commander, Major Alston-Roberts-West. Amongst the wounded, Arthur Rice was safely evacuated, along with Les Drinkwater, who was himself hit by shellfire after arriving at the Regimental Aid Post with Rice; both men survived the war. The Coldstream suffered two officers and twenty men killed or missing while the 2/North Staffs lost six officers and men from A Company. It was during the course of this battle that Bootle-Wilbraham remembered with some irony receiving an order of the day from the Commander-in-Chief, 'in which he said the British Army had to withdraw through no fault of its own and was to now stand and fight on the line of the [Escaut]'.

Chapter Four

I Corps on the Escaut

During the withdrawal from the River Dendre Lieutenant General Michael Barker's three divisions had retreated along one road. Communication between brigade and division was almost non-existent and delayed messages were contradicted by new orders that themselves were often rescinded as British and French units became inextricably muddled. The result was a confusion of misunderstandings as to who was to be deployed where. Certainly inadequate staff work was largely responsible for the 2nd Division being squeezed in between the 42nd and 48th Divisions, with the unfortunate 6 Brigade originally ordered to hold the river line between Chercq and Calonne. On arrival they found units of 126 Brigade from the 42nd Division already in possession of part of the sector, resulting in the 126 Brigade units remaining and 6 Brigade moving into reserve at Willemeau. As Bell remarked in his *History of the Manchester Regiment*, it was 'quite impossible to trace all the consequences of the orders and counter-orders that were issued to the three brigades' [of the 2nd Division] on 20 May'.

The 42nd Division
In 1937 Major General William Holmes became the British Army's youngest major general at the age of 45 and in 1938 was appointed to command the Territorial 42nd (East Lancashire) Division. On 16 May the two remaining brigades of the division (127 Brigade was diverted to Macforce the same day) were ordered to Tournai to take up defensive positions on both sides of the Escaut. In 1940 the Escaut at Tournai was markedly different from the river today. Apart from being much narrower, the river formed a loop at the Faubourg-de-Marie through the north-eastern half of the city to rejoin the main channel near the prison. This two mile loop was called the *Petite Rivière* and was crossed by numerous bridges, giving the 1/East Lancashires (126 Brigade) the unenviable task of destroying a multitude of crossing points.

Initially, HQ of the 5/Border Regiment (126 Brigade), which was under the command of Lieutenant Colonel Hugh Law, was situated to the north-west of the city in Château de Beauregard at Froyennes. Keeping

Tournai was badly bombed in 1940 as this photograph of the destroyed archives demonstrates.

D Company in reserve at Froyennes, Law deployed A Company to guard the bridges in the city and B and C Companies to the eastern outskirts some two miles beyond the *Petit Rivière*. On the night of 16 May the Luftwaffe heavily bombed Tournai, leaving much of the city in flames, the 5/Border war diary commenting that there were very few civilian firemen left to fight the fires.

On 19 May Law moved Battalion HQ a little further south to La Marmite and was reinforced by the 1/Border Regiment (125 Brigade). The first indication the British had of the approaching German 18th Division was when units of the French First Army began to fall back across the Escaut, which was followed by an officer from I Corps HQ with orders for the demolition of the last remaining bridge. The immediate necessity of this was hotly disputed by the 1/East Lancashire bridge party but, finally adhering to orders, the bridge was destroyed at 7.00pm, an exercise which left the 1st Division rearguard cut off on the wrong side of the river. Fortunately most of the rearguard did manage to get back but Captain Anthony Lewis of the 1/Royal Welch Fusiliers was shot dead by the enemy after swimming the river to make contact with the stranded units.

There was little chance of holding the German assault troop for very long and by late on 21 May they had broken through the 1/Border positions in the north of the city. Recovering quickly, Brigadier George Sutton sent orders for the 1/6 Lancashire Fusiliers to counter-attack and restore the positions. Crossing the start line at 11.00am without any artillery support, A and C Company's advanced as far as the railway embankment where they ground to a halt in the face of furious enemy fire. Intent on regaining the line of the river, Lieutenant Colonel James Gartside – who had won an MC with the Irish Guards in the previous war – ordered up Lieutenant Bill Nelson and the Carrier Platoon to head a second attack. Launched at 8.15pm with three companies of infantry, there was no stopping the Fusiliers assault, which drove the enemy back across the river as well as taking twenty-five prisoners together with a quantity of arms and equipment. There is an almost regretful note made on 22 May by the Lancashire Fusiliers historian: 'On the afternoon of the next day orders were received to the effect that the division was withdrawing to previously prepared positions (a phrase much heard in those days) in the area of Grunston, south of Lille, with 125 Brigade in divisional reserve'.

The 2nd Division

It was in the I Corps sector that another VC was awarded south of Tournai where the 2/Norfolks, under the command of Major Nicholas Charlton, had positioned three companies along the river frontage just south of Tournai down to Chercq. Charlton had only been in command since 18 May after Gerald de Wilton had been evacuated after a nervous breakdown and was at this time installed with the rest of Battalion Headquarters in Château de Curgies on the outskirts of Calonne. The Norfolks and 1/8 Lancashire Fusiliers had at least arrived in time to relieve 6 Brigade before the German assault began, a scenario that was unfortunately not repeated further south at Calonne.

Deployed on the right flank of the Norfolks' sector – with some of his platoon positions in the grounds of Château de Chartreaux – Captain Peter Barclay – who had been awarded the MC for his patrol work on the Maginot line – had established the remainder of his men in the cover of buildings along the river. Private Ernie Leggett remembered his section was

Captain Peter Barclay commanded A Company of the 2/Royal Norfolks.

The Château de Curgies in 1940.

concealed extremely well amongst the ruins of an old cement factory. It was from these hidden positions that Barclay and the men of A Company observed German infantry making a determined effort to cross the water by laying wooden hurdles across the rubble of the demolished bridge:

> *I reckoned we'd wait until there were as many as we could contend with on our side of the canal before opening fire. There were SS with black helmets and they started to come across and were standing about in little groups waiting. When we'd enough, about 25, I blew my hunting horn. Then of course all the soldiers opened fire with consummate accuracy and disposed of all the enemy personnel on our side of the canal and also the ones on the bank at the far side – which brought the hostile proceedings to an abrupt halt.*

The accuracy of the resulting artillery and mortar fire indicated to Barclay that the German gunners had guessed correctly as to their positions and were now using their superior fire power to prelude a more serious river crossing. This same bombardment was also searching the battalion's rear areas; a lucky round succeeding in hitting the Norfolks' HQ at Calonne, wounding Charlton, his Adjutant and Intelligence Officer, leaving the battalion in the hands of Major Lisle Ryder. It was around this time that Barclay was wounded in the stomach and thigh and, with no stretcher available, his batman, despite Barclay's protests, tied him to a door, resulting in a very disgruntled but badly wounded officer to deal with 'a very threatening situation' almost completely immobile! Barclay later conceded his batman's actions had probably saved his life.

Barclay had spotted German infantry who were now crossing the river on the company's right flank where there appeared to be no defending infantry to deal with the threat. In spite of the rising number of casualties being taken by the company, he hit back with the meagre reserves available to him – the company clerk, radio operator and other personnel from Company Headquarters – led by Sergeant Major George Gristock, with orders to cover the flank and deal with a German machine gun that had established itself not very far off on the company's right flank. Barclay's plan was tinged with a hint of desperation and he had no idea it would result in the award of a VC. But it worked:

> *He [Gristock] placed some of his men in position to curtail the activities of the post so effectively that they wiped them out. While this was going on, fire came from another German post on our side of the canal. Gristock spotted where this was and he left two*

men to give him covering fire. He went forward with a Tommy gun and grenades to dispose of this party, which was in position behind a pile of stones on the bank of the canal itself. When he was about 20-30 yards from this position, which hadn't seen him, he was spotted by another machine gun post on the enemy's side. They opened fire on him and raked him through – smashed both knees. In spite of this he dragged himself till he was within grenade lobbing range, then lay on his side and lobbed the grenade over the pile of stones [and] *belted the three Germans.*

The arrival of the Norfolks' reserve company secured the right flank and Barclay and Gristock were evacuated to the Regimental Aid Post. The battalion war diary makes no mention of Gristock's action or his award of the Victoria Cross, which was announced in the *London Gazette* of 23 August – sadly, after Gristock's death.

Sharing a corner of the RAP with George Gristock was Ernie Leggett, who had been badly wounded in the cement factory by enemy mortar fire. Initially left for dead, he was rescued by 'Lance Corporal John Woodrow and a chap named 'Bunt' Bloxham'. Fortunately all three men were got away well before the orders were received on 22 May to retire to the Gort Line. Gristock and Leggett would meet again in the Royal County Hospital at Brighton, where Leggett was horrified to learn the CSM had both legs amputated at the hip. 'I used to stay with him for half an hour or an hour. Every day they'd wheel me through. Then that horrible morning came on 16 June when they hadn't come and got me.'

Company Sergeant Major George Gristock VC.

48th Division

Some of the most desperate fighting along the Escaut was on the 48th Divisional front, south of Tournai, where Major General 'Bulgy' Thorne – a former Grenadier Guards officer who had fought with the 1st Battalion at Geluvelt in 1914 – must have despaired at the indecisiveness displayed by General Barker and his staff as they struggled to deploy I Corps. There is no doubt that the delay in relieving the territorial battalions of 143 Brigade resulted in disastrous consequences for the 8/Royal Warwicks, who were still on the Escaut long after Lieutenant Colonel Harold Money and the 1/Royal Scots had arrived to take over the 1/7 Warwick's positions on the night of 20 May.

The 1/7 Warwicks, under Lieutenant Colonel Gerard Mole's command, were a little to the north of Calonne, holding a front of some 1,000 yards, with two companies deployed in buildings along the river and two in reserve on the sloping ground to the west. The 8th Battalion was in and to the south of Calonne and held a slightly longer frontage, again amongst buildings along the river side. Lieutenant Colonel Reginald Baker moved three companies forward, keeping D Company in reserve at Battalion Headquarters at Warnaffles Farm. The regular 2nd Battalion from 144 Brigade, under the command of Lieutenant Colonel Piers Dunn, was at Hollain, where the battalion adjutant, Captain Dick Tomes, thought the battalion's position on the river was too open on the right flank and provided the enemy with a 'covered approach' on the left:

> *We had sunk some barges the day before but the stream* [Escaut] *was not wide, only some 30 yards. The ground was flat by the river and the slope on which the town of Hollain stood, which did in fact overlook the far bank in a few places, was not adaptable to defence on account of the houses; we could not have stopped the crossing of the river from it.*

Although there had been some contact the previous day, the battle increased in intensity during the morning of 20 May. At Hollain German infantry from the 253rd Division began crossing in the afternoon under the cover of intense shelling, making their most determined effort opposite D Company, where a sharp bend in the river offered more concealment – exactly the point where Tomes had anticipated the enemy might give them trouble. Tomes' account tells us this was largely thwarted although, 'a few men with LMGs had succeeded in gaining a foothold on our side and were shooting from gardens in front of A Company'. By the time darkness fell the battalion was still holding its positions.

On the 1/7 Battalion front a number of men had been killed or wounded by enemy shellfire before the relief by the 1/Royal Scots went ahead as planned, although enemy shellfire did give Harold Money some anxious moments before the battalion were established at midnight. However, much to the grief of the 8/Warwicks, the intended relief by the 2/Dorsets never took place. All the evidence points towards the confusion of 'orders and counter-orders' that had dogged the Dorsets on 20 May; so much so that by early the next morning the battalion was still east of St Maur, attempting to extricate themselves from a mix-up of units from 4 Brigade, which were 'milling around in the early morning mist'.

In the meantime the 8/Warwicks were having a hard time in the face of enemy mortar and machine gun fire, one casualty being the battalion medical officer, Captain Neil Robinson, who was killed whilst loading wounded into an ambulance. Battalion Headquarters and the B Echelon transport also came under fire; but the forward companies did manage to prevent the enemy from crossing the river after dark – or thought they had. At midnight a C Company patrol was fired upon from a building on the west bank; evidently units of IR 54 had managed to gain a foothold and were on the west bank. Darkness also meant that any relief that might have been planned could not now take place until the following night. Lieutenant Colonel Baker's men resigned themselves to another day of hard fighting.

The 21 May was, in the words of the Royal Scots Adjutant, Major James Bruce, 'a hellish day! We were mortared and shelled heavily.' The nearby enemy lodgement on the 8/Warwicks' C Company front was also proving troublesome but not as much as the pressure on the battalion's left flank was giving B Company. Under cover of the now standard high explosive bombardment, some enemy did manage to get across but were dealt with quickly by the carriers and bayonets of the Royal Scots. However, despite the efforts of their neighbours, the Warwicks' forward companies were slowly pushed back into an enclave on the edge of Calonne, giving further opportunity to the IR 54 Infantry to cross at the junction of A and B Companies. The situation now hung in the balance. The surviving Warwicks were all but cut off from Battalion Headquarters and were in great danger of envelopment. Decisive action was needed and quickly.

The officers of the 2/Royal Warwicks taken at Rumegies in January 1940. Second left Captain Dick Tomes, fourth left Lieutenant Colonel Piers Dunn.

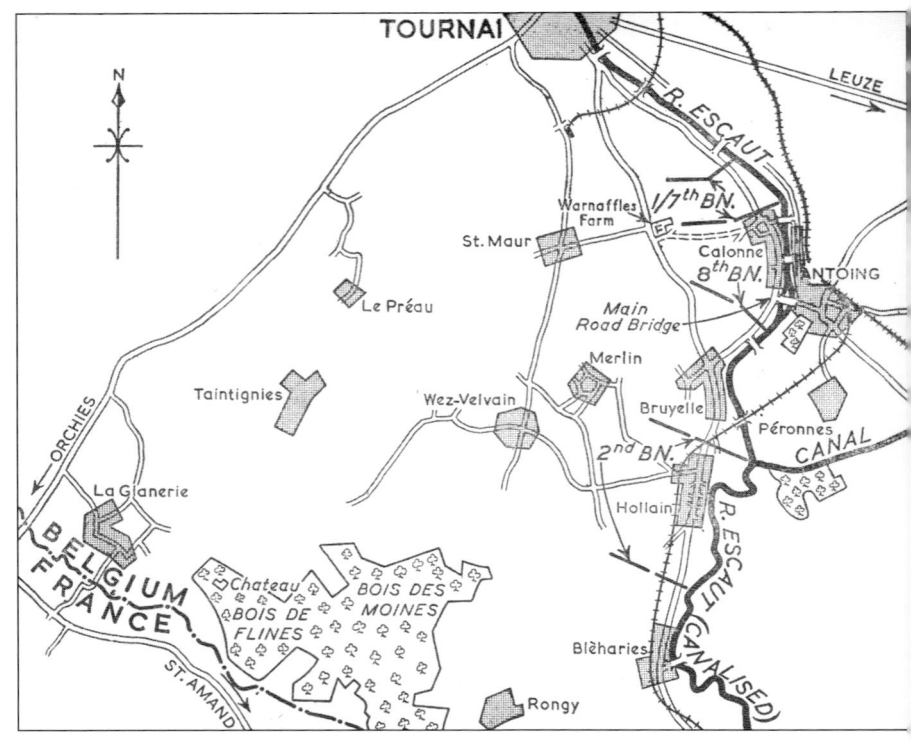

A map taken from *The History of the Royal Warwickshire Regiment* showing the location of the three Royal Warwickshire battalions.

The action led by Lieutenant Colonel Baker was certainly decisive but whether his decision to lead the attack himself was altogether wise is open to debate. Instead of bringing his reserve company into the fight, he assembled an attacking force from Battalion Headquarters and led them towards an enemy who were now firmly established on the west bank in some strength. Captain Neil Holdich, commanding C Company of the 1/7 Warwicks, felt the whole exercise to be several hours too late:

> Now followed one of the most fantastic affairs since the Light Brigade, albeit on a much smaller scale. Their C.O. removed his helmet

Captain Neil Holdich 1/7 Royal Warwicks.

52

and equipment, put on his orange and blue regimental forage cap, took up his swagger stick and formed up the men of his Battalion H.Q. in one extended arrowhead on the open ground behind Calonne. Himself at 'point', and supported by a couple of Bren Gun Carriers, the whole show moved like part of a peacetime Tattoo towards the village. As they descended the slope into the village, the carrier's guns ceased to bear on the enemy and, unhindered, the Germans blazed away. It was all over very quickly, a crash of flame and smoke and all went, three officers [sic]and 50 men, only two surviving.

In actual fact there were five officers killed in what can only be described as a disaster. Baker was killed along with his men, leaving the British dead strewn across the battlefield and only two survivors returning to Warnaffles Farm. Undoubtedly courageous, Baker's attack had made very little difference to the situation apart from depriving the battalion of its commanding officer and a number of valuable men.

The 1/Cameron Highlanders counter-attack later in the morning did managed to partially re-establish the line, which certainly eased the lot of the Royal Scots. Captain Ronald Leah, commanding B Company, recalled being 'shelled all the way between Merlin and the main road' over ground that was unpleasantly exposed. From Leah's account it would appear that his company headquarters was situated in the wooded area around Château de Lannoy and the B Company platoons formed up on either side of the Rue de L'Aire. With their objective the small bridge

The Château de Lannoy.

near the cement works, Leah's men managed to clear the broken ground behind the works – although he says the area was a 'death trap'; with 12 Platoon losing a lot of men. The attack hit Leah's company very hard and he was particularly saddened by the death of Lieutenant Peter Grant, his second in command. Yet it may well have been the Cameron Highlanders' counter attack – together with the dogged resistance elsewhere – that finally saw the Germans being pulled back over the canal that night, a retirement that allowed the surviving 8/Royal Warwicks to begin retiring. Although more rejoined later, that evening at roll call only 366 men answered their names.

On the 2/Royal Warwicks' front 21 May opened with another determined attack on D Company's positions resulting in enemy troops gaining what Dick Tomes termed as 'a considerable footing on our side of the river'. Shortly after this a runner arrived at Battalion Headquarters with the news that Major Phillip Morley had been killed leading an attack on a German machine gun post – leaving 21-year-old Second Lieutenant Kenneth Hope-Jones in command of the company. The attack on D Company was renewed just after midday and, although they held on to their positions, enemy troops managed to get into the small wood immediately behind them. Relief arrived in the form of a counter attack by three companies of the 1/Ox and Bucks:

> *The plan entailed B Company advancing 15 minutes ahead of the remaining companies to secure the right flank of the attack, a*

German injured being treated under fire.

difficult task which was carried out at some cost, including another very good young officer, Second Lieutenant [George] *Duncan. The carriers supported the attack from the west while the 3-inch mortars fired a hundred bombs into the wood.*

As far as Dick Tomes was concerned, the attack came at just the right moment:

With the assistance of A Company's covering fire [they] *drove the enemy back a considerable distance – though not over the river – and captured about a dozen prisoners. But D Company suffered heavily and the remaining two subalterns, Hope-Jones and Goodliffe,* [Goodliffe was later found to have survived], *and a great many men had been killed. PSM Perkins was wounded and later died, together with the majority of his platoon taken prisoner. No officers and 30 men remained out of two platoons.*

The situation around Calonne still remained tense despite the numerous counter-attacks that appeared to contain enemy incursions; but the constant pressure and superior fire power from an enemy intent on crossing the river was taking its toll.

On the right flank of the 2/Royal Warwicks were the three battalions of 145 Brigade. The 2/Gloucesters, commanded by Major Maurice Gilmore, were sandwiched between the 2/Royal Warwicks on their left and the 4/Ox and Bucks Light Infantry on their right, Brigadier Nigel Somerset opting to keep the 1/Buckinghamshires in reserve at Lesdain, where he established Brigade HQ. According to the Rev David Wild, chaplain to the 4/Ox and Bucks, it was:

A drab, treeless place, consisting of two main streets running parallel to each other. Joining these two was a short street fifty yards long ... When the German artillery came into action the church spire was such an obvious aiming mark that this little street behind became a very unhealthy corner.

The Gloucesters were still smarting from an air attack on their convoy at Ramecroix, where they were caught almost totally by surprise and lost nearly 200 men killed and wounded. Two of the five vehicles that were hit were carrying troops. Captain Bill Wilson, commanding B Company, felt the attack 'was the inevitable result of travelling in daylight'. Gilmore established his HQ in an estaminet near the Y-junction north-west of Jollain-Merlin. The 4/Ox and Bucks took up their positions at Bléharies,

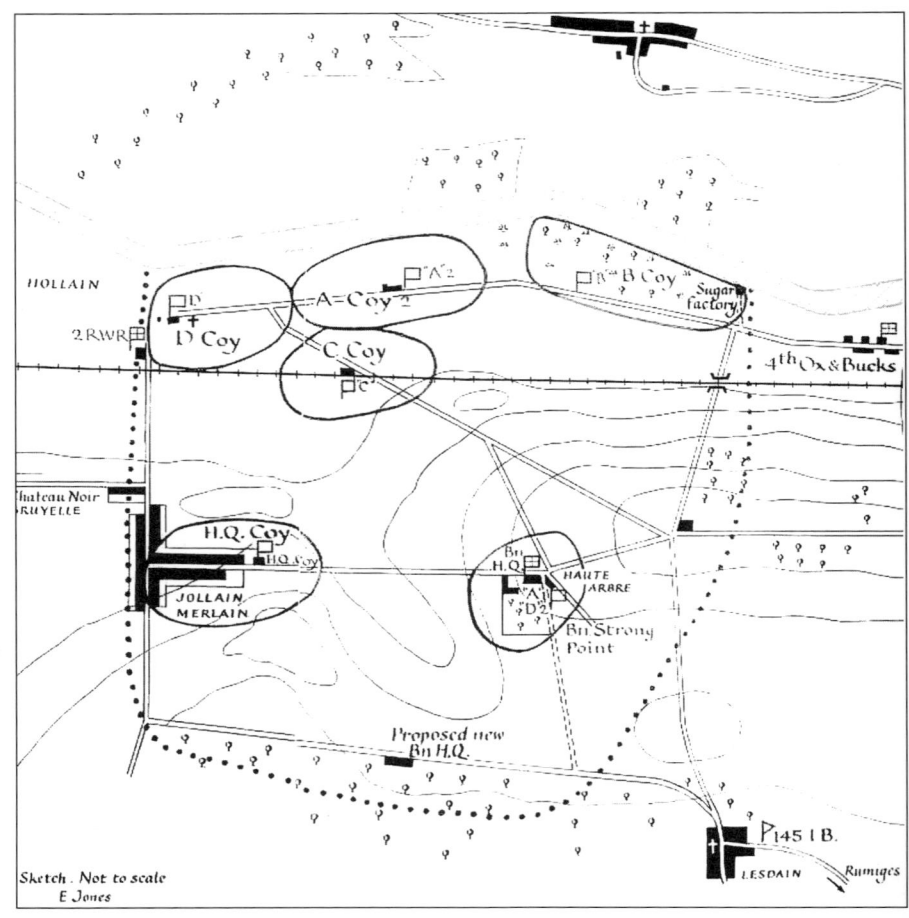

A sketch map drawn by Eric Jones depicting the 2 Gloucesters' deployment at Bruyelle

with A and D Companies holding the line of the Escaut and B and C Companies in reserve, Battalion HQ was in the village itself. On 20 May Lieutenant Colonel Geoffrey Kennedy pulled his companies back to a new line behind what he called 'a subsidiary canal'. Compared to the fighting further north the battalion had a relatively peaceful few days on the Escaut, although there was 'considerable artillery activity on both sides'. Enemy gunners appeared to focus their attentions on destroying the village while the British gunners shelled lines of communication and villages on the eastern side of the river. The village of Sin came in for particular attention and was almost entirely destroyed.

That is not to say there was no German activity. Lance Corporal Turner recalled that B Company's area was positioned between the railway embankment and the canal, with the mortar section sited just behind them and screened to some extent by the embankment:

> *Just before dark* [20 May] *Jerry launched a vigorous attack and attempted to cross the water. He was supported by very little artillery. Our gunners, on the other bank, rose to the occasion and plastered the area between the canal and the wood with a most effective rain of shells ... That night was very noisy, but despite his efforts Jerry did not cross the canal alive and his casualties appeared to be heavy.*

The enemy footholds gained along the Escaut – however small – were disturbing enough; but the breakthrough on the 44th Division front at Oudenaarde had compromised the whole of the Escaut Line, leaving Gort and his commanders in a sticky situation. As with the BEF units further north, instructions ordering the withdrawal on arrived 22 May and set in motion the retirement from the I Corps sector, which was 'successfully carried out', wrote Harold Money, 'to the accompaniment of mortars, shells and last, but not least, the song of the Nightingales singing as though to drown out the former'. Nevertheless, the Royal Scots had been hit hard, losing over 150 men, one of whom was the battalion's second

The bridge at Bléharies prior to its demolition in 1940. Note the width of the Escaut at this point.

in command, Major George Byam-Shaw, who had been frozen to his Bren gun five months previously on the Maginot Line.

The decision to abandon the Escaut was confirmed at the GHQ conference at Brooke's headquarters at Wambrechies in the late afternoon of 21 May which, according to Brooke, was marked by Gort's rather gloomy account of the situation facing the BEF. The Arras counter-stroke had failed, the Germans were reported to be close to Boulogne and there were enormous difficulties in the resupply of ammunition to the fighting divisions. 'We decided', wrote Brooke, 'that we should have to come back to the line of the frontier defences tomorrow evening. Namely to occupy the defences we spent the winter preparing'; Brooke's diary does not mention if the possibility of a British evacuation from the channel ports was discussed at this meeting; but Gort and his commanders must have been aware that the likelihood of the BEF remaining on the French mainland was fast becoming unrealistic.

Chapter Five

Artillery on the Escaut

The defence of the Escaut was probably one of the last occasions during the 1940 France and Flanders campaign when artillery was used in a formal battleground framework along a designated front. Thereafter, the speed of the retreat often forced the gunners into independent actions, where they were constantly supporting a variety of infantry formations and reacting to orders that were usually out of date almost before they had been acted upon. What is perhaps not always appreciated is the gunners were continuously fighting or supporting infantry rearguard actions as the BEF fell back on the channel ports. However, it must be said that the BEF was in little position to maintain a static defence with its mixture of obsolete and modern weaponry, in what had been described as the 'pot-pourri of equipment' available to the gunners.

Development after the First World War was limited by a lack of money; however, it was agreed that a new design was necessary and this came about from converting the existing stock of 18-pounders. Where funds were available a new 25-pounder barrel and gun carriage was introduced, which left many older 18-pounders still in service and generally allocated to the Territorial artillery units. Lieutenant Noel James, an officer with 68/Field Regiment, wrote of his dismay when their guns were replaced in September 1939:

> *These were 18-pounders Mark II as used in the First World War and on their breech blocks was stamped the date, '1917'. The only apparent modification which had been carried out was the substitution of the large wooden wheels with small steel ones, which were fitted with pneumatic tyres, but these guns were very different to the Mark IVs which they replaced.*

In September 1939 many of the Royal Artillery (RA) field regiments had still not been issued with anti-tank rounds for the 25-pounder field gun, ammunition for the 2-pounder anti-tank gun was limited and the medium artillery regiments were still, in the main, equipped with the obsolete 6-inch howitzer. Lessons learned during the First World War, in particular

A 25-pounder gun being towed by a Light Dragon artillery tractor.

that standardised equipment was crucial for battlefield success, had been forgotten in the economically challenging and pacifist inter-war years.

In 1940 divisional artillery brigades were under the overall command of the Commander Royal Artillery (CRA), who was usually a brigadier and worked closely with the divisional infantry commander. Each artillery brigade consisted of three field regiments, each commanded by a lieutenant colonel, and containing two batteries of guns. Each battery, under the command of a major, comprised three troops of four guns of 18 or 25-pounders and with a complement of 200 officer and men. Thus, on paper, each divisional artillery brigade would have seventy-two guns. In addition, each brigade of artillery had an anti-tank regiment of forty-eight 2-pounder anti-tank guns or, in some cases, the 25mm French Hotchkiss anti-tank gun. Organised into four batteries of twelve guns, these units were usually deployed to individual infantry brigades. Characteristic of this operational organisation was the 2nd Divisional Artillery, commanded by Brigadier Charles Findlay, which consisted of

10, 16 and 99/Field Regiments along with 13/Anti-Tank Regiment. On the Escaut Findlay worked closely with Major General Noel Irwin, who took command of the division on 20 May.

Each of the three corps commanders delegated the allocation and movement of the artillery units held in corps reserve to their Corps Commander Royal Artillery. The corps reserve consisted of anti-aircraft batteries, medium army field regiments armed with 60-pounder guns and heavy and super heavy regiments, which were equipped with 6-inch or 8-inch howitzers. It was quite normal for the CRA to allocate one field regiment to each brigade of infantry, although divisional commanders usually asked for, and received, further artillery units from corps reserve.

By 1940 infantry brigades were quite accustomed to forward observation officers (FOOs) controlling the use of artillery through direct communication with batteries. At battalion level the battery commander would work with the battalion commander through the FOO, who was able to call down an artillery bombardment on specific locations. Typical of this was the action reported by Captain Dick Tomes of the 2/Royal Warwicks at Hollain, when the guns of 24/Field Regiment were directed to fire on 'several columns of vehicles and guns' on the eastern side of the Escaut. Tomes wrote that 'our artillery was very thick on the ground and was a cheering sight'. The use of FOOs was the result of a system

Men of the 2/Essex Regiment with a Hotchkiss 25mm anti-tank gun.

first introduced during the First World War, when indirect fire was used in the Aisne Valley in the latter part of 1914. But, as they discovered in 1914, it was a hazardous occupation.

Several FOOs were either killed or wounded while manning observation posts (OP) on the Escaut, particularly if they were positioned in church towers and industrial buildings, as they often were south of Tournai. 68/Field Regiment, for example, reported engaging German infantry crossing the Escaut at 3.00pm on 21 May. Their FOO was Captain Gordon Potts, who had gone into the 2/Gloucester's sector at Bruyelle to establish his OP, was located by enemy gunners and killed on 21 May. Another FOO from 16/Field Regiment, Lieutenant Shaw, was wounded near Antoing whilst observing and bringing fire down on small groups of enemy infantry attempting to cross the river. On 22 May 115, 140 and 10/Field Regiments, who were in positions around Warnaffles Farm and St Maur, were in action firing on German incursions in the Calonne area. Directing fire from his OP near St Maur, Captain Tim Mead was killed on 20 May by enemy shell fire. The 115/Field Regiment war diary commented on the excellent work carried out by Mead before his death, an opinion that was echoed by Lieutenant Colonel Harold Money of the 1/Royal Scots. 18/Field Regiment, who had their guns at Guignies, were fortunate in having six observations posts along the ridge of high ground between St Maur and the river. The regiment fired some 2,000 rounds over a forty-eight hour period but sadly lost Lieutenant Arthur Someren, who was killed while calling for artillery support on German units attempting to cross the river. The18/Field Regiment war diary remarked that Gunner Healy was awarded the MM for maintaining the telephone lines back to St Maur.

Lieutenant Ronald Baxter, a troop commander with 367/Battery, 140/Field Regiment, manning an OP near St Maur – very possibly close to Tim Mead's position – overlooking the river and was tasked with plotting the flashes from enemy guns and reporting their position to the battery. His account of being under fire from German batteries would have been an experience endured by many officers and men manning OPs. Although the ground in front of him sloped away, he could not see the river but was able to see the far side and the German positions. Shortly before dawn on 20 May a battery from 115/Field Regiment came into action close by:

> *Soon this brought down enemy fire on St Maur and the troop* [F Troop 140/Field Regiment] *itself. I clearly saw shells exploding amongst the houses. I heard later that some guns were lost and casualties were suffered amongst the crews ... Then the German gunners gave their attention to the wood I was in, starting on the*

left and working along. Now we were for it. There were three of us in the OP with only a shallow six foot trench for protection ... Bits and pieces of trees and shells flew in all directions but thanks to our slit in the earth we escaped unscathed. My overcoat and webbing equipment were hanging on a tree beside the hole we were in. The hem of the coat was torn and holed and the equipment hit by splinters. A rifle, leaning against another tree nearby, had its stock shattered.

But FOOs were not always in evidence. The 2/Grenadier Guards at Helkjin were subjected to a heavy and prolonged enemy bombardment that began at 7.30am on 20 May, with the battalion war diary caustically remarking that 'there was no liaison between batteries and forward batteries and no FOOs were to be found'. Perhaps even more alarming was the blunt statement that the German batteries could not be engaged by our supporting artillery 'as they had orders not to fire until the enemy crossed the river owing to the extreme shortage of ammunition, not was any counter-battery fire permitted'.

Further north the 2/Lancashire Fusiliers reported the battalion, supported by a troop of 30/Field Regiment, inflicted numerous casualties on formed bodies of enemy moving forward to the river. Whether a FOO was involved in this action was not mentioned; but the enemy reply, which came soon afterwards, indicated an almost endless supply of ammunition:

At about 2pm the enemy put down a series of heavy artillery concentrations, the accuracy of their artillery fire being remarkable. Battalion Headquarters, A Company and B Company suffered most, whilst the DCLI on our right and the East Surreys and Queen's on our left also got heavily shelled. The bombardment lasted until approximately 6.00pm.

On 22 May The 1/Loyals at Pont-a-Chin noted that 'our own artillery was now limited to five rounds a day per gun', which did little to placate the battalion commander when he learned that twenty of his men were killed and wounded when the D Company HQ was demolished by a single German shell. Nevertheless, while these reports of 'concentrated' German bombardments abound in British accounts of the battle, the German artillery in fact seldom concentrated their artillery; their advantage lay in the abundance of ammunition available to them, together with very effective mortar fire and air superiority, debunking to some extent the British notion that logistics and mobility were more important than firepower.

The Westland Lysander had a crew of two and came into service in 1938.

Contemporary accounts of the 1940 fighting often describe captured British and French aircraft appearing over positions on the Escaut which – although not realised at the time – were clearly spotting for German artillery batteries. The RAF had designated the Westland Lysander to work with the artillery regiments but this appeared to be an unsuccessful partnership. There had been several problems with the slow moving and obsolescent Lysander and the few attempts that were made to conduct air to ground shoots had resulted in German fighters driving it away or the destruction of the aircraft and, very often, the crew as well. It is a sad fact that over 115 Lysanders were lost over France and Belgium during the 1940 campaign. Consequently, most artillery observation was carried out by FOOs.

10/Field Regiment complained bitterly that 'the Boche seemed to have complete air superiority' and with it 'the uninterrupted ability to spot for their own artillery'. B Company of the 1/5 Queen's were only too well aware of this when they took up positions on the high ground north of Petegem on 21 May where they were immediately spotted by a German aircraft, soon after which 'heavy salvos were brought on to them'. Lieutenant Colonel Boxshall, commanding the 1/East Surreys, recalls it was low flying German aircraft that directed an artillery bombardment on the battalion positions on 21 May, the two shells that landed on Battalion HQ killing four and wounding several others.

The *Luftwaffe* may have had air superiority but that did not prevent the 52/Light Anti-Aircraft Regiment, under the command of Lieutenant Colonel Charles Mather, from making their mark around Tournai on 18 May, where it shot down two Dorniers and two Heinkels. Possibly the most successful anti-aircraft regiment in the BEF, over the course of the campaign the regiment was credited with fifty-eight confirmed kills and another thirty-seven aircraft almost certainly shot down or disabled.

Captured aircraft were, in the opinion of many on the Escaut, an absolute menace. The regimental historian of the Beds and Herts Regiment reported that on the 20 May a Lysander reconnaissance aircraft flew low over the battalion positions

> *It was possible to see the pilot and observer clearly. What was not appreciated at the time was that in all probability the aircraft had been captured by the Germans and they were plotting our positions. This was evident during the course of the day when enemy artillery fire was directed against our lines of communication and on roads running through Avelgem.*

Second Lieutenant Anthony Irwin of the 2/Essex recalled another occasion when a Lysander spotting for a British battery was targeted by six Me109s. To the amazement of Irwin and the men of C Company, the Lysander pilot embarked upon a display of flying that not only avoided the attentions of the Me109s but reduced one of Irwin's men to tears of relief as the 'Lizzie' remained airborne:

> *The Huns returned and changed their tactics. They split up and attacked all at once from different directions. They should have had her cold but, as they opened up, she climbed, stalled and spun towards our position. The Hun followed her down, thinking she [the Lysander] was a gonner. She straightened up, pulled out of the spin and raced across our orchard, tipping the tops of the trees. The Huns, not seeing us, followed close after.*

A furious barrage of fire from C Company's nine Bren guns hit the first aircraft and forced the remaining five to rethink their strategy. Irwin remarked later that it was only the intervention of three Hurricanes that prevented the Me109s from exacting their revenge on the clustered ground troops below and 'the Lizzie was in the air again half an hour later'.

Sadly, successes like these were few and far between and, as far as the Royal Artillery was concerned, one of the only positive elements to have emerged from the 1940 campaign was the programme of re-equipment that was forced upon them by the loss of so much material in France. It has often been said that from the disaster of Dunkirk rose the awesome firepower that proved so decisive after 1942.

That said, there were of course numerous occasions where artillery played a decisive part in holding back the advancing German forces while the bulk of the BEF was evacuated from the channel ports. At Hazebrouck it was the guns of 98/Field Regiment that played a significant role against the 8th Panzer Division while the Royal Horse Artillery at Hondeghem propelled themselves into legend with their defence of the town against the German 4/Rifle Battalion. Both these, and the gallant defence of Cassel, are described in detail in the Battleground Europe volume *Cassel and Hazebrouck 1940*.

Chapter Six

The Tours

This section contains the usual advice to visitors and has divided the sector into four car tours that take the battlefield tourist from Oudenaarde in the north to Warnaffles Farm in the south; a distance of some sixty miles. In addition there are two short walks that explore the battlefield in greater detail.

Using the guide and advice to visitors
In order to fully appreciate a battleground and what took place it is essential to get out on the ground and walk in the footsteps of history. This guide has been written with that purpose in mind and, to that end, includes several opportunities to leave the vehicle behind and walk the ground on which the BEF fought in May 1940. Although the area is largely industrialised south of Tournai, the northern part of the sector, which includes the 'Flemish Ardennes', with its network of cycle and pedestrian tracks, is a most attractive part of Belgium. South of Tournai the Escaut takes on a more industrialized mantle and although the urban archaeology from many years of cement manufacture have been erased through landscaping and development there are still many reminders of its industrial past, with ancient lime kilns punctuating the ground bordering the river. That said, walkers can still occasionally find themselves off the beaten track and should take the necessary precautions against inclement weather.

Maps
While simple route maps for walkers can be found in the text, there are no drawn maps for the car tours. These are best supported by the directions given in each tour and the Belgian IGN 1:100,000 maps, which can be purchased at most good tourist offices and online from www.mapsworldwide.com. However, bear in mind that satellite navigation can be a very useful supplement in supporting general route finding, particularly when trying to locate obscure CWGC cemeteries. For the walker the larger scale IGN 1:25,000 Series maps can be also bought in Belgium or online, while the Michelin Travel Partner Map can

be downloaded free onto your IPad. Finally, the author would highly recommend using Google Earth or the French *Géoportail* for preparatory work prior to visiting the area.

Travel and where to stay
By far the quickest passage across the Channel is via the Tunnel at Folkstone, the thirty six minutes travelling time comparing favourably with the longer ferry journey from Dover. Whether your choice of route is over or under the Channel, early booking well in advance is always recommended if advantage is to be taken of the cheaper fares.

Travel time from **Calais** to **Tournai** is approximately one and a half hours – depending on traffic conditions – using the A16 and A25 motorways. If you are intending to base yourself in Tournai there is a plethora of hotels and bed and breakfast accommodation available on the internet but the author enjoyed his stay at the three-star **Hotel d'Alcantara** on Rue des Bouchers St Jacques, which is near the city centre. Tournai is certainly worth a visit if only to visit the twelfth century Notre Dame Cathedral, which dominates the skyline of the surrounding area. Further information can be obtained from the Tourist Office in the Place Paul-Emile Janson, which is near the cathedral.

If you are using **Oudenaarde** as a base it may be more appropriate to use the A19 via Kortrijk, a journey which will take approximately one hour fifty minutes by car, depending on traffic conditions. Oudenaarde abounds with hotels and bed and breakfast accommodation, all of which can be found on the internet. The author has personal experience of the three-star **Hotel Cesar** in the Markt, which has a good restaurant and includes breakfast in the price. The town itself is steeped in history and hosts several memorials from both world wars on either side of the Tacambaroplein, which is a short walk from the Markt. Further information can be obtained at the Tourist Information Centre and Museum, both of which are located in the fourteenth century Stadhuis in the Markt. Please bear in mind that Thursday is market day.

Driving abroad is not the expedition it was years ago and most battlefield visitors these days may well have already made the journey several times. However, if this is the first time you have ventured on French and Belgian roads there are one or two common sense rules to take into consideration. Ensure your vehicle is properly insured and covered by suitable breakdown insurance; if in doubt contact your insurer, who will advise you. There are also a number of compulsory items to be carried by motorists that are required by French law. These include your driving licence and vehicle registration documents, a warning triangle, a *Conformité Européenne* (CE) approved fluorescent safety vest, headlamp beam convertors and the visible display of a GB plate. Whereas some modern cars have built in headlamp convertors and many have a GB plate incorporated into the rear number plate, French law also requires the vehicle to be equipped with a first aid kit, a fire extinguisher and a breath test kit. Possibly, the law is currently vague (2016). If you fail to have these available there are some hefty on the spot fines for these motoring offences if caught driving without them. Most, if not all, of these items can be purchased at the various outlets at the Tunnel and the channel port at Dover and on board the ferries themselves.

Driving on the 'wrong side of the road' can pose some challenges. Here are three tips that the author has always found useful:

1. When driving on single carriageway roads try to stop at petrol stations on the right hand side of the road. It is much more natural then to continue driving on the right hand side of the road after you leave. Leaving a garage or supermarket is often the time when you find yourself naturally turning onto the wrong side of the road.
2. Take your time! Don't rush! If you rush your instinct may take over and your instinct is geared to driving on the left.
3. Pay particular care on roundabouts. A lot of drivers do not and rarely appear to use indicators. Navigators remember to look at the signs anti-clockwise and drivers remember that the danger is coming from the left. On a more personal note it is always advisable to ensure that your E111 Card is valid in addition to any personal accident insurance you may have; and have a supply of any medication that you may be taking at the time.

Visiting Commonwealth War Graves Commission Cemeteries

Most of the cemeteries referred to in this guide are located in churchyards or communal cemeteries; only two of the cemeteries we visit are dedicated Commonwealth War Graves Commission (CWGC) cemeteries. Almost all the communal and churchyard cemeteries you will discover in this area share their ground with casualties from the final months of the 1914-1918 War.

The concept of the Imperial War Graves Commission (IWGC) was created by Major Fabian Ware, the volunteer leader of a Red

Fabian Ware became vice-president of the IWGC in 1917.

Cross mobile unit that saw service on the Western Front for most of the period of the First World War. Concern for the identification and burial of the dead led him to lobby for an organization devoted to burial and maintenance of the graves of those killed or who had died in the service of their country. This led to the Prince of Wales becoming the president of the IWGC in May 1917, with Ware as his vice president. Forty-three years later the IWGC became the Commonwealth War Graves Commission. The commission was responsible for introducing the standardized headstone that brought equality in death regardless of rank, race or creed; and it is this familiar white headstone that you will see now in CWGC cemeteries all over the world. Where there is a CWGC plot within a communal or churchyard cemetery the familiar green and white sign at the entrance, with the words *Tombes de Guerre du Commonwealth* or *Oologsgraven van het Gemenebest* in Flemish, will indicate their presence. The tall Cross of Sacrifice with the bronze Crusader's sword can be found in the larger cemeteries and a visitor's book and register of casualties is usually kept in the bronze box by the entrance. This may be absent from some of the smaller cemeteries. Cemetery details can be found at the end of the appropriate car tour.

Car Tour 1

Oudenaarde to Elsegem

Start – The bridge at Eine
Finish – Château d'Elsegem
Distance – Eleven miles including some optional walking

This tour covers the 44th Divisional area, from Eine in the north to Château d'Elsegem (Kwaadestraat Château) in the south-west and focuses on the German breakthrough at Huiwede and their subsequent advance to take the high ground around Knok and Anzegem. We begin north of Oudenaarde at the Eine Bridge, which is the seventh bridge to be built at this crossing point. The first bridge, which was constructed in 1881, was destroyed by the Belgian army in 1914. The second bridge was destroyed by the Germans in November 1918 to prevent the allied advance across the Escaut, while the third was constructed days later by the American 37th Division, who made a difficult and costly crossing of the Escaut in their pursuit of the Germans. The fourth bridge, named the

One of the present day bison on the approaches to the Eine road bridge.

The original plaque commemorating the American advance in 1918 still bears shrapnel scars from 1940.

Ohio Bridge, was constructed in 1928/9 by the Americans in memory of the fallen of the 37th (Ohio) Division and was adorned with two bison on each of the approaches to the bridge. A symbol of strength and courage, the bison were sculpted by Paul Moreau-Vauthier. On 19 May 1940 the bridge was held by B Company of the 5/RWK and was destroyed at 5.30pm by 210/Field Company, Royal Engineers, after an air attack that left three men dead and one missing. A replacement pontoon bridge was built by the Germans in October 1940. The sixth bridge was begun in 1952 and opened two years later, with new bison sculpted by Jos de Decker. This bridge was destroyed in 1982 during the widening of the river and the new, larger bridge with its bison that you see today was finally opened on 25 June 1982.

> Cross the bridge and continue into Nederename to pick up the N46, which will take you under the railway line to Ename, where 210/Field Company demolished the railway bridge on 19 May, and south to Oudenaarde. At the junction with the N453 turn right and then, after one hundred yards, left into Bergstraat. A little further along you will cross a road bridge with a car park immediately on the left. Turn in here to park and walk across to the bridge.

This is the Egypten Bridge and is the last remaining bridge of the three 1940 bridges over the Escaut at Oudenaarde. The realignment of the Escaut removed the south-eastern loop of the river, apart from the narrow stretch of water you can still see on the northern side of the bridge. The discarded loop was filled in and now follows the line of the cycle and pedestrian pathway – Trekweg Rechterover – which you can see running behind the car park. In May 1940 the 5/RWK were deployed from the north eastern edge of Oudenaarde to the Eine Bridge, with their battalion headquarters at Diepenbeke. Arriving with the remainder of 132 Brigade on 14 May, the battalion, under the command of Lieutenant Colonel Evan Kerr, took up its position on the right of Lieutenant Colonel Chitty's 4/RWK, who were based in Oudenaarde. The 1/RWK, under the command of Lieutenant Colonel Evelyn Sharpin, were kept in reserve around Eekhout and Moregem.

The 4/RWK forward positions on either side of the bridge, together with the railway station in the north of the town, were attacked by the *Luftwaffe* on 19 May, causing about twenty casualties in A and B Company, who were positioned either side of the bridge. The regimental historian tells us that the right hand bridge carrying the railway was

The truncated loop of the Escaut at the one remaining bridge of 1940 vintage in Oudenaarde.

damaged and houses on either side were set alight. The air raid prompted Brigadier James Steele, commanding 132 Brigade, to order the bridges crossing the Escaut to be blown later that day by the 210/Field Company sappers.

> From the bridge continue into Oudenaarde over the Escaut to the Markt, where you will pass the imposing tower of St Walburga Church, which dominates the town.

This may be a good time to visit the museum in the Stadhuis, where you can see an excellent visual display of the various stages of development that have altered the course of the Escaut. The Museum is open during the summer months, Tuesday to Sunday, from 10.00am to 5.30pm. From October to February, opening hours are from 10.00am to 5.00pm Tuesday to Friday, with half day opening at weekends. The Tourist information Office is next to the Museum.

> From the Markt head north-west towards Moregem on a route which will eventually take you out of the town along the Kortrijkse Heerweg. This minor road will take you to the front gates of Moregem Château (Kasteelwijk Château as described by the 4/RWK historian). There is parking by the gate from where you can see the building, which is now in an advanced state of decay and is almost completely surrounded by trees.

The magnificent Stadhuis at Oudenaarde.

Moregem (Kasteelwijk) Château is unoccupied and in poor condition.

This was the 4/RWK Battalion HQ and where D Company were initially kept in reserve, although Chitty does mention later moving to an advanced 'battle' HQ in a windmill nearer the river. The château came under heavy attack as German forces advanced north; on one occasion an incendiary bomb came through a window, prompting Lance Corporal Edward Culmer to pick it up and throw it back. He was awarded the MM for his coolness under fire.

Sergeant Frank Jezzard tells us that at 4.00pm he was at the château and was prevented from leaving on 22 May by heavy German shelling and machine gun fire. His account of the escape from the château suggests that Major Marcus Keane, who commanded the rearguard, had already been killed and command had devolved to PSM Arthur Chapman, who was later awarded the DCM for his leadership. Jezzard writes that 'between ourselves we decided to make a break for it when darkness came as it was suicide to make an attempt in daylight'. Arriving at the main gates of the château, it was quickly decided to leave from the back of the château grounds, a route that would have taken them north to the Wortegem Road. There are still shrapnel marks to be seen on the pillars of the main gates.

The gatehouse and front entrance to Moregem Château still bear shrapnel marks from 1940.

> Continue into Moregem and park outside the church. The headquarters of 132 Brigade was situated in the village and the 1/RWK HQ was at a nearby farm. You may wish to stop briefly here to visit the churchyard cemetery. From Moregem head south to Eekhout, where the Lindestraat will take you to the former Petegem railway station. Almost immediately after crossing the railway line turn left and park in Clemmenstraat.

This level crossing became quite critical on 21 May after the German advance from the Escaut through Petegem succeeded in forcing Lieutenant Frazer of the 1/RWK and the men of his platoon out of the burning station buildings and back to Eekhout, where the defending garrison under Captain Victor Warr managed to hold the German advance before he was evacuated and died of his wounds. Later that morning Brigadier Steele ordered a counter-attack on Petegem, which was carried out by the

Brigadier James Steele commanded 132 Brigade.

reserve companies of the 1st and 4th Battalions, together with two carrier sections from the 4/RWK. Led by Captain David Archer and D Company, the station at Petegem was recaptured; but the attack failed to link up with C Company of 2/Buffs in Petegem village. Steele ordered another counter-attack by A Company 1/RWK to seize a section of the railway line east of the station – which from where you are is towards the lorry depot at the end of Clemmenstraat. This attack was successful and A Company dug in next to the Buffs.

By nightfall on 21 May the German bridgehead included De Motte, Petegem and much of the open ground between Petegem and Oudenaarde. Eekhout and the railway line were still in British hands, but Eekhout had become a salient. On 22 May Eekhout was badly bombed and gradually, to the accompaniment of shell fire and strengthening German forces, the thin British line was forced back towards Moregem Château.

> From the level crossing continue through Petegem until you reach the junction with the N453. Turn left and park.

The former site of Petegem railway station.

Petegem crossroads, where Major Lord Edward Sysonby's carrier attack turned left towards the church.

If you turn round and look south-west along the N453 you will be looking in the direction, from which Major Lord Edward Sysonby and his carriers from 1/5 Queens Royal Regiment (West Surreys) approached the crossroads at dawn on 21 May. Advancing to the crossroads, Sysonby's men turned left and came face to face with a column of marching German infantry. Somewhere along the main street, between the junction and the church, Sysonby shot a German infantryman in the face with his revolver. Turning round, the carriers brought a withering fire down on the surprised Germans before they withdrew.

> Continue for thirty yards and take the next turning on the right – Muurstraat – which will take you along a narrow road to Huiwede. Park by the junction of tracks and take the opportunity to stretch your legs.

Across to your right are the buildings associated with Beaulieu Abbey and the former convent that was destroyed in 1786. Today only the gatehouse and a few buildings have survived. The château with its round tower is – at the time of writing – for sale, but in May 1940 it housed the headquarters of D Company of the 2/Buffs. Behind you are the houses of Huiwede village and to your right, concealed amidst the trees and shrubs, is Seheldtekant Château, which was in the 1/6 Queens sector.

The ground you are now standing on was defended by the 2/Buffs, who were relying to some extent on the drainage canal of the Rietgracht to prevent any German armoured excursion. Walk down towards the river by taking the right hand track, which will take you across the Rietgracht before it swings round to the right to reach the tow path. Across the river you can see the church at Melden and the high ground where German troops were first seen by the 2/Buffs' outposts. Leave the tow path and continue past an information board and over a small bridge to reach a more substantial path in the Scheldehoek Golf Terrain. On your right is the now redundant section of the old river. It was in this area, where the river formed a pronounced loop, that German forces crossed during the night of 20 May under the cover of a heavy artillery and mortar bombardment.

The 2/Buffs war diary tells us that at about 9.00pm on 20 May, about a hundred Germans were seen on the far bank and, having crossed the

Beaulieu Château, which housed the headquarters of D Company of the 2/Buffs.

Part of the former loop of the Escaut where German forces crossed on the night of 21 May.

river by inflatable boats, engaged 8 Platoon of A Company. It was from here that German infantry moved up to Huiwede, which was defended by A Company of the 2/Buffs under Major Bruce, with D Company and Major Ransley on their right flank. C Company, under Major Rowe, was further to the east, with their HQ in a farm near the N453. B Company was in reserve in and around Petegem. Walk back up the track to Huiwede.

By 9.45pm the left platoon of D Company had been driven back and 8 and 9 Platoons began to withdraw. This was the point at which Brigadier John Utterson-Kelso, commanding 131 Brigade, ordered B Company of the 2/Buffs to move across to their right, with Captain Francis Crozier in command, in support of the 1/6 Queen's. In retrospect this was probably a mistake, as without the support from B Company Major Bruce and the men of A Company were forced out of Huiwede to the higher ground to the north.

Brigadier John Utterson-Kelso then ordered a counter-attack to retake the village. A tall order when you consider it was dark and the whole battlefield was masked in a shroud of confusion! The counter-attack was launched at 2.30am on 21 May and led by B Company 1/RWK with one company and a couple of sections of the carrier platoon from the 1/5 Queen's in support. Despite the outskirts of the village being entered twice by the British, both attacks failed in a confusion of firing and faulty orders. The darkness played into the hands of the attackers and allowed German infantry not only to reinforce their foothold at Huiwede but to penetrate the houses at the eastern end of Petegem. The casualties from this counter-attack included Major Bruce, who was wounded and taken prisoner. The 1/5 Queen's carriers then moved north to join Major Sysonsby in the attack on Petegem.

> From Huiwede return to the T-junction with the N453 and turn left. Continue for 600 yards until you see the entrance to the Oudenaarde Golf and Country Club on the left. Turn down here and follow the road past the magnificent Petegem Château (referred to as Scheldekant Château in regimental histories) to the car park. Although this is a private members club, the author has never had any difficulty in using the car park and walking round the outside of the château, although it is always advisable to seek permission at reception.

This magnificent neo Renaissance style château was built by Baron August Pyke in 1847, who was then living nearby in the moated château which stands some 350 yards further to the west and marked *Oud Kasteel*

Huiwede is still a small hamlet today, with a handful of private houses clustered along a single roadway.

Scheldekant Château is now the preserve of the Oudenaarde Golf and Country Club.

on IGN maps. In 1940 the Oud Kasteel was uninhabited and partly in ruins and was bought by the present owners in 1997 and who have restored it to its former glory. You will pass this building on the way to the Domein de Ghellink.

In May 1940 the 1/6 Queen's, under the command of Lieutenant Colonel Ivor Hughes, held a 3,000 yard sector of the river from Scheldekant Château to the hamlet of Eeuhoek inclusive. C Company occupied the Scheldekant Château grounds, although it is unclear whether the château building was temporarily occupied by Captain Reginald Pontifex and the C Company HQ staff. On Pontifex's right were A and B Companies, with D Company in reserve in the Elsegem Château (referred to as the Kwaadestraat Château in regimental histories, which we will visit later). At 3.00pm on 21 May large groups of German infantry were seen moving through the woods to the south of the château where 14 Platoon, under 21-year-old Second Lieutenant Geoffrey Worke's command, was the first to come into contact. Worke was killed in this engagement, along with Captain Pontifex, who died when C Company was overrun at 5.30pm.

Leave the château car park and turn left along the minor road past the moated château on the left and follow the road round to the right to pass through the now disused gates. Continue to the T-junction with the N453 and turn left. We are now going to visit the former Château d'Elsegem, the remnants of which are to be found in the Domein de Ghellink. The turning to the former château grounds is approximately one mile further along the N453, on the left hand side. After turning down the entrance avenue leave your vehicle in the car park and walk down towards the river.

By 8.00pm on 21 May German units had reached Elsegem and were firing into the rear of the château grounds. The 1/6 Queen's Battalion HQ was situated in a lodge in the north-west corner of the château grounds and drove off the first German attacks; but amongst the casualties was the battalion's second in command, Major Bevington, who was badly wounded. D Company by this time were fully committed and the battle in the grounds – where you are standing now – was left to B Company of the 1/5 Queen's, who had been drafted in as reinforcements, and HQ Company of the 1/6 Queens. By 10.15pm that evening, after B Company had been overwhelmed, Lieutenant Colonel Hughes and the survivors, covered by C Company of the 1/5 Queen's, began to withdraw towards Anzegem.

The restored moated château originally occupied by Baron August Pyke.

The Domein de Ghellink, where a modern day restaurant and exhibition building now stand.

Nothing remains of the Château d'Elsegem, which was burnt down in 1974.

The site of the former château is behind the restaurant building. The once grand building stood surrounded by the moat and was crossed by a bridge, over which you can still walk. Sadly, all that remains after the fire of 1973 are the foundations on which the large canvass structure now stands.

CEMETERIES
Oudenaarde Communal Cemetery
Situated in the eastern side of the town of Groenstraat, there are eighteen Second World War burials here, including one unidentified casualty, who may be a casualty of the 19 May *Luftwaffe* attack at Oudenaarde, along with those from 210/Field Company and 65/Field Regiment. The seven casualties from the 1914-18 conflict are mostly of men who died as prisoners of war. The 429 Squadron crew were killed when Halifax LW415 was shot down on 2 May 1944 by a night fighter. The pilot was thrown out of the exploding aircraft and subsequently evaded capture. **Sergeants Victor Foy** and **Charles Gardener** from 626 Squadron were killed when their Lancaster ND985 was shot down on 28 May 1944 by a night fighter when returning from Aachen. The pilot and one of the air gunners are buried at Courtrai.

Oudenaarde Communal Cemetery.

The church at Moregem and the churchyard cemetery.

Moregem Churchyard
There are two Second World War burials in this churchyard cemetery, which you will find in the centre of the village. **Private Arthur Woollaston** MM from the 4/RWK and 18-year-old **Sapper Dennis Harriott** from 210/Field Company are buried close together. Harriott may well be another casualty of the *Luftwaffe* attack on the Escaut bridges in Oudenaarde on 19 May. **Second Lieutenant Thomas Coughlan** of the 3/Royal Irish Fusiliers was killed eighteen days before the Armistice was declared on 11 November 1918.

Anzegem Communal Cemetery
The cemetery is best approached from the N382, where an access road leads to a car park. There are eighteen Second World War burials here, which you can find to the right of the main entrance. Buried alone is the single grave of **Corporal Edward Crocker** of the 10/RWK, who was killed four days before the Armistice of 11 November 1918. Buried next

to each other are two men of the 8/Middlesex machine gunners, 19-year-old **Second Lieutenant Ion Grove-White,** who died of wounds on 21 May 1940 and **Corporal Fred Charles,** who died of wounds on 30 June. The three men of the 4/Royal Sussex – 133 Brigade – were killed by shellfire near Waregem on 21 May after a captured Lysander was seen spotting for the German batteries. The 7 Squadron crew of Lancaster JB455 died when their aircraft crashed after bombing railway yards at Lens and Valenciennes. The pilot, **Pilot Officer Jones**, evaded capture.

Car Tour 2

Kaster to Escanaffles

Start – Kaster Churchyard
Finish – The bridge at Escanaffles
Distance – Ten miles including some optional walking

This tour looks in more detail at the ground held by the 4th Division and can be linked with Car Tour 1 by using the N453 and the N382 to Kaster. The tour begins at the church at Kaster, which is east of the N383 at the end of Juliaan Claerhoutstraat. There is plenty of parking here to allow you to visit the churchyard cemetery. Kaster was also the initial location of the 1/East Surreys Battalion HQ and it is their sector that we are now going to visit.

After leaving the cemetery, turn left at the junction with the main road and continue down the N36 into Kerkhove. Cross the bridge over the Escaut towards Berchem, turn right on the bend and park in Kerkstraat. Walk back across the bridge and stop when you are halfway across.

The first thing to bear in mind here is the Escaut today looks nothing like it did in 1940. The realignment of the river has moved the waterway south of its original path and the 1940 bridge, which was demolished by 7/Field Company on 20 May, bears no resemblance to the modern bridge you are standing on. That aside, it takes little imagination to see where Lieutenant Colonel Reginald Boxhall deployed A Company in Kerkove to defend the bridge, with B Company on their left holding the flat ground of the river bank you can see to the right of the bridge. If you turn round and face Berchem it becomes a little more difficult to visualise where Boxhall positioned his two other companies, as Berchem in 1940 was little more than a crossroads. The Regimental historian simply says 'C and D Companies were in positions on the eastern side of the river, under Major Hambleton Bousefield, in and around the village of Bercham'. Ahead of you the high ground of Mont de l'Enclus, which so worried Boxhall, should be visible, while to your left the high ground opposite Oudenaarde at Melden can be seen.

It was on the eastern edge of Berchem village that A Company of

The new road bridge at Kerkove looking north from Berchem.

5/Northamptons, under the command of Captain Hart, were dug in and came into contact with the German cyclists. The remaining three companies of Northamptons were defending some 2000 yards of river bank on the western side. D Company, on the battalion's left flank, was in touch with the Queen's in the 44th Division and B Company was in reserve at Kerkove, along with Battalion HQ. If you look over the railings of the bridge you will have some idea of what it must have been like for C and D Companies of the East Surreys and D Company of the 5/Northamptons to paddle across to the Kerkove bank of the river after the bridge had been blown.

Now turn and face Kerkhove. With his battalion now on the western side, Colonel Boxhall moved his HQ nearer the river and deployed A, B and C Companies along it, with C Company in reserve about 300 yards behind. As enemy shell fire increased, the forward positions of the East Surreys and Northamptons began to take casualties; but any German movement across the river was prevented. Of course by this time the Germans had begun their advance north from Huiwede in the 44th Divisional area, an incursion that was impacting on the Northamptons' positions. Lieutenant Colonel Bill Green, commanding the Northamptons, had little choice but to drastically alter his battalion's positions:

> *D Company stood firm against any efforts to widen the* [Huiwede] *bridgehead, but suffered considerable casualties from the enemy's fire and, by the end of the day, their effective strength was less than two platoons. Shortly before midnight, therefore, the Battalion front was readjusted. A Company were moved up to the left of C Company, and D Company were withdrawn slightly to link up with the left of A Company. The front being roughly in the shape of a right angle with the left flank thrown back from the river to meet the threat caused by the* [44th Division].

During the night of 21 May the 6/Black Watch from 12 Brigade took up position on the Northampton's left to prevent the Germans working round and surrounding them.

At 3.00pm on the 22nd the Germans launched a full scale assault and made successful crossings at several points; but at the demolished Kerkove bridge they were unsuccessful, thanks to a counter-attack led by Captain Rickets that temporarily restored the status quo at this point but left Ricketts badly wounded in the process. At 4.30pm the Northamptons were ordered to withdraw, the same message reaching the East Surreys at 6.00pm. It was while the two battalions were breaking contact with the enemy that Lieutenant Colonel Bill Green was killed.

> Return to your vehicle and cross the bridge to Kerkhove to turn left at the roundabout along the N8 to Waamaarde. In a little under a mile turn right at the crossroads along Onze-Lieve Vrouwstraat, where you will see the church on the left. There is plenty of parking a few yards further along on the right. As you walk towards the Escaut you will cross a small bridge over the Rijtgracht. Continue for 200 yards until you reach the river bank. In 1940 a ferry operated from this spot.

This is the 2/Lancashire Fusiliers' sector where Lieutenant Colonel Leslie Rougier deployed A Company on the right flank, with B and C Companies defending the river bank, leaving D Company in reserve. Apart from the forward section posts along the bank of the river, Rougier's main force was positioned behind the Rijtgracht. Battalion HQ was established about half a mile south of Tiegem. The German artillery bombardment that began on the morning of 21 May was devastatingly accurate, with A and C Companies suffering heavy casualties. Major Manley, the battalion second in command, recalls an enemy observation balloon was up all afternoon which, together with frequent visits from the *Luftwaffe,* made life very uncomfortable:

The church at Waarmaarde.

The night of 21/22 May and the morning of 22 May the enemy artillery and mortar fire continued and there was an exchange of small arms fire on both sides. The enemy were known to be over the canal [sic] *on our left and the positions were looking somewhat precarious. At about 2.00pm on 22 May heavy enemy concentrations of artillery were put down on the whole divisional front ... The enemy could be seen moving forwards to the canal and again we inflicted many casualties. At about 3.00pm it was reported that our right flank had been left open and the enemy had broken through. The Commanding Officer sent up the Carrier Platoon under Captain Hugh Woollatt to form a defensive flank on A Company's right.*

At 6.15pm orders from Brigade HQ finally arrived ordering the battalion to retire; but it was probably Woollatt's action that saved the day, allowing the Fusiliers a window of respite in which to withdraw to the comparative safety of the Tiegem Ridge. Sadly, half a mile from the ridge, Leslie Rougier was hit by shellfire and killed.

Retrace your steps across the Rijtgracht to the churchyard. After visiting the cemetery in the churchyard – the CWGC plot is on the right at the back of the cemetery – continue to the T-junction with the N8 and turn left. We are now going to visit the bridge at Rugge, which is best approached by driving along the N8 for a further 1.15 miles and turning left down Ruggesstraat. After 270 yards you will find a car park on the right where, should you wish to stretch your legs, you can leave the car. From your vehicle it is just over half a mile to the bridge on Avelgemstraat.

This is the ground defended by the 2/DCLI, who arrived from Alost on 19 May. As you either walk or drive up to the bridge you will pass over the Rijtgracht drainage waterway. Apart from widening, the course of the river between Rugge and Escanaffles has changed very little. As you approach the bridge – which is still in the approximate position it was in May 1940 – you will get some idea of the difficulty Lieutenant Colonel Eric Rushton faced when deploying his battalion along the river. The first thing to notice is the embankment carrying the approach road to the bridge, which formed a barrier between positions on either side,

The new road bridge at Rugge.

Today the Rijtgracht is almost redundant and only fills during heavy rain.

effectively preventing any mutual fire support. Secondly, the almost complete absence of cover made movement beyond the Rijtgracht almost impossible during the day as the whole of the position was overlooked by the German held Mont de l'Enclus, which you can see almost directly ahead of you. Rushton was therefore forced to deploy the bulk of his men behind the Rijtgracht – some 600 yards north-west of the river.

After you arrive on the bridge look back towards Rugge. Having retired behind the Rijtgracht, the battalion was extended for about a mile either side of the town, with C Company on the right flank (your left if looking from the bridge) and linking up with Lieutenant Colonel Birch's Bedfords. D Company was in occupation of the town and B Company was in touch with the 2/Lancashire Fusiliers at Waarmaarde on the left flank. Rushton kept Captain Pentreath and A Company in reserve. Although the war diary gives no specific date and time, it would appear the bridge was blown on 20 May.

The main German attack began on 21 May, when an attempted crossing was held by the battalion and the guns of 22/Field Regiment. Rugge itself came in for a particularly heavy enemy bombardment and by dusk only one building appeared to have escaped damage. Late on 21 May, reports that the enemy had gained control of the bridge prompted Pentreath's three man patrol to discover the exact nature of the German positions. Even by today's standards the success of this audacious patrol was an outstanding achievement. The bridge was eventually destroyed by the officer commanding 157/Battery from 53/Light Anti-Aircraft Regiment.

> Return to the junction with the N8 and turn left. Our next stop is Avelgem, which is approximately one mile further along the road. On arriving at the crossroads you will find Kerkstraat on your left with the church at the far end. There is plenty of parking here should you wish to stop.

This is where Lieutenant Colonel Birch, commanding the 2/Bedfordshire and Hertfordshires, established his HQ near these crossroads on the Heestert road – now called Neerstraat – and where Birch met with Brigadier Evelyn Barker on 19 May in what Birch describes as a 'cafe at the crossroads'.

The crossroads at Avelgem. Lieutenant Colonel Birch established his HQ along the road to the left.

The former railway station at Avelgem today.

From the crossroads continue south along the N8 for another 650 yards until you reach the former railway station in Yzerwegstraat. Stop here.

Initially, Birch deployed three companies on the river, with C Company holding the bridgehead at Escanaffles with support from some anti-tank guns. The bridge was blown on 19 May but, as Birch wrote later, 'It was a grand explosion and a good demolition, but it was possible for a man to crawl over the canal on the debris'. Faced with the same dilemma as Rushton, with the 'billiard table' ground between the river and the town offering little cover and overlooked by the Mont de l'Enclus, Birch decided to withdraw the battalion behind the Rijtgracht, leaving the forward posts close to the canal.

After the bridge at Escanaffles had been demolished, C Company were initially positioned on the eastern side of the railway station before Birch moved them to the west side, near the goods yard and road bridge. If you walk towards the industrial buildings for 140 yards to the end of Vijverhoek you will be standing where the bridge crossed the railway line in the vicinity of the goods yard. On 19 May the CQMS had established the battalion cookers in the station yard, where everyone was fed prior to their deployment.

The station building remains largely as it was in May 1940.

> The site of the railway bridge, which Birch reports was blown sometime before they arrived, can be reached by walking to the N353 at the eastern end of the former railway station. On the far side of the road, by the pedestrian crossing, a track leads south-east towards the river. Follow the track for 0.74 miles to where it joins the towpath. This is where the railway line crossed the river.

You can still see the former bridging point and across the river is the continuation of the railway embankment. D Company was positioned here on the western side of the railway embankment and it was from this point that Second Lieutenant Cart de Lafontaine, commanding 13 Platoon, crossed the river to reconnoitre the buildings on the far side. Incredibly, he returned unscathed. Shortly after this Birch withdrew the battalion – apart from some section posts – north of the Rijtgracht, which you will have crossed while walking along the old railway line. It is likely that D Company used this route when they withdrew. Walk back to your vehicle.

> Drive down to the bridge at Escanaffles and park on the far side where there is some verge side parking.

The bridge was held on the far side by C Company, with orders to hold it until all friendly troops had passed but to blow the structure if it looked like it would fall into enemy hands. One can only imagine the scene as Lance Corporal Major and his section doubled back across the bridge minutes before the bridge erupted in a confusion of debris, some of it landing by the estaminet that had been taken over as C Company HQ and was only some two hundred yards from the bridge. The owner had

The bridge at Escanaffles that was demolished in May 1940.

The new bridge over the Escaut at Escanaffles constructed after the river was widened.

decided to leave the previous day after emptying his beer barrels but, fortunately, enough beer was found to toast the explosion!

After the battalion was withdrawn to the line of the Rijtgracht, the Germans attempted to filter men over the blown bridge to form a bridgehead. The ensuing counter-attack led by Second Lieutenant David Muirhead and 15 Platoon would have approached using the narrow road from Avelgem before attacking the bridge from a flank. Twelve minutes was allowed for Muirhead's men to arrive on the bridge before the guns of 22/Field Regiment would lift onto Escanaffles. The attack was completely successful. Second Lieutenant Lafontaine's platoon, who were giving fire support from the river bank, reported the German infantry retired almost immediately the guns open fire.

CEMETERIES
Kaster Churchyard

The cemetery is located next to the church in the Juliaan Claerhoutstraat and contains seventeen Second World War casualties, two of whom are unidentified. Of the seven identified men of the 1/East Surreys, who were all killed between 21 and 22 May, three were married men and all hailed from the London area, one of these being 27-year-old **Sergeant James**

Sergeant James Hannington, 1st Battalion East Surrey Regiment.

The CWGC plot at Waamaarde Churchyard.

Hannington, who lived with his wife, Harriet, in Acton, London and was killed on 21 May.

Waarmaarde Churchyard
The cemetery is next to the church on Onze-Lieve Vrouwstraat and contains eighteen Second World War casualties, of whom one is unidentified. There are also two unidentified burials from the First World War. The most senior is 44-year-old **Lieutenant Colonel Charles Leslie Rougier**, who was killed on 22 May during the retirement of the 2/Lancashire Fusiliers from the Escaut. Rougier was awarded the Military Cross in 1918 and lies in the cemetery along with sixteen of his men, a number which includes **Fusilier John Worsley**, who was awarded the Military Medal for his part in a fighting patrol in March 1940.

Ingoyghem Military Cemetery
The village of Ingoyghem is northwest of Tiegem and was taken by the 9th (Scottish) Division in October 1918, which accounts for the high

number of British and German 1918 burials here. Once in the village, follow the CWGC signposts from the N36 to Sint-Antoniusstraat, where you will find the triangular shaped cemetery on the right. The one casualty from 1916 – Canadian born **Flight Sub Lieutenant Kenneth van Allen** – died of wounds after his Caudron G.IV from 5 Wing Royal Naval Air Service crashed in May 1916. There are three burials from the Second World War, one of which is unidentified. **Gunner Bernard Jones,** from 69/Medium Regiment, Royal Artillery, was killed on 21 May and 21-year-old **Private David Burke,** of the 6/Black Watch, died between 22 May and 1 June 1940.

Avelgem Communal Cemetery
The village is approached along the N8 from Rugge. After 0.74 miles, where the road bends round to the left, you will see a road on the right signposted Otegem. Turn here to bear left at the next two junctions to follow Kerkhofstraat for just over one mile until you see the cemetery on the right. There are twenty-six casualties from the Second World War buried here, three of whom are unidentified. Walk up the central avenue and the CWGC plot is on the right near a large tree. The fourteen casualties from the 1/6 East Surreys were largely suffered after the battalion relieved the 2/DCLI on 21 May. Private Arthur Hitchcock's diary recalled 'many casualties from shelling and mortar fire as the battalion withdrew'. **Second Lieutenant Robert Emmett** was killed by a sniper while attempting to support a patrol led by Second Lieutenant John Williams, while **PSM Richard Harris** was one of several men who were killed by mortar fire when their platoon HQ was hit. The battalion's two days on the Escaut was a very costly one. The 19-year-old **Second Lieutenant Gordon Medway,** of the 2/Beds and Herts, was killed when a shell landed in the A Company trenches. The epitaph on the headstone of **Second Lieutenant John Haye** – *His was a heart that held its life-blood cheap to shed in England's cause* – is the first line from a poem that that now hangs in the DCLI Regimental Museum, in Bodmin, Cornwall. He was killed by shellfire after the battalion had pulled back behind the Rijtgracht.

Second Lieutenant Gordon Medway.

Car Tour 3

Helkijn to Tournai

Start – The bridge at Helkijn
Finish – Tournai Communal Cemetery, Allied Extension
Distance – Twenty-one miles

This tour begins in the 3rd Divisional area, moves south to look at the 1st Division around Pecq, before concluding at Tournai Communal Cemetery. It can also be combined with Car Tour 2. We begin at the bridge at Helkijn, which is in the sector defended by 7 (Guards) Brigade and best approached using the N353 to Helkijn. A left turn onto Kerkstraat will take you through the village to the bridge on Brugstraat. Alternatively, you can park by the church and walk the last 500 yards. The modern day road bridge is not in exactly the same position as it was in 1940 as the post-war widening and realignment of the Escaut moved the course of the river approximately sixty yards further to the south.

The modern day bridge at Helkijn.

The bridge was defended by the 2/Grenadier Guards, who had orders to hold the bridge at all costs until 8 Infantry Brigade had crossed. Consequently Lieutenant Colonel Lloyd placed No.1 and No.3 Companies on the eastern side, with No.2 Company on the bridge, holding No.4 Company in reserve ready to counter-attack if necessary. Battalion HQ was established in a small estaminet on the western side of the river until it was moved back to a new position on the edge of the village. The battalion had not arrived until quite late in the day but the war diary notes that all companies were in position by about 7.00pm on 19 May. These were tense hours for the Grenadiers but 8 Brigade finally crossed the river and the bridge was demolished at 2.00am on 20 May.

It was only after the bridge had been blown that Major Colvin was able to allocate company positions on the western bank for the defence of Helkijn. With little other choice, Major General Bernard Montgomery had deployed all three of the 3rd Division's brigades along the river. 7 (Guards) Brigade had 9 Brigade on its left flank (the ground to the right of Helkijn if you are looking from the bridge) and 8 Brigade on the right flank, where they were in touch with the 2/Coldstream Guards around Pecq. It was the sector at Helkijn that saw the most determined assault on the British positions, as German infantry repeatedly tried to cross using the demolished bridge on 20 May. But with assistance from the 1/Coldstream, the sector was held until Lloyd's Grenadiers were withdrawn on 22 May.

> Retrace your steps back to the churchyard, where 20-year-old **Guardsman Francis Sheppard** will appreciate a visit before you continue to the T-junction with the N353 and turn left towards Spiere (Esperierres). Continue for 1.14 miles until you see a narrow road on the left – Sluisweg – leading down to Lock Number 4, where there is parking.

You have just travelled along the sector held by 1/Grenadier Guards, which ran from the sugar factory on the outskirts of Helkijn – seen on the left as you leave the village – to the junction of the Escaut with the Canal de l'Espierres. Where you are now was the sector held by No.4 Company which, in May 1940, contained the only access to the river from the eastern bank via a large dam and the lock you can see in front of you. It was not possible to demolish this structure because of the adverse effects it would have on water levels in the river. This is the point from which **Lieutenant Bill Pritchard** and a demolition party from 246/Field Company crossed the river and blew up five buildings that were obscuring the Grenadiers' field of fire. They were covered

Sappers of the Royal Engineers were worked hard during the retreat, demolishing bridges and other structures.

from the western bank by **Second Lieutenant Gore-Browne** and his platoon. Bill Pritchard was quite familiar with explosives having already blown up a pontoon bridge under fire on 16 May, for which he had the dubious honour of being the first Territorial officer to be the awarded the MC in the war.

Retrace your steps to the N353 and turn left into Spiere. Château d'Espeirres, which was the battalion HQ of the 1/Grenadiers, is still in private hands and in 1940 was the property of the Baron de Fosse et d'Espierres. According to the war diary, the château possessed a very strong cellar but little, if any, of this rather magnificent building can be viewed from the road. Continue along the N353 through Warcoing to Pecq, passing the Communal Cemetery on the left. Turn right at the crossroads onto the N510 for approximately 300 yards and park near the large school building (École Moyenne) on the right.

The École Moyenne at Pecq billeted two battalions of 1 (Guards) Brigade on 19 May.

Pecq was part of the 1st Divisional sector and had been allocated to the 2/Coldstream Guards under the command of Lieutenant Colonel Lionel Bootle-Wilbraham. His original orders were for 1 (Guards) Brigade to hold a sector running from Pont-a-Chin to Pecq, with the 3/Grenadiers on the right, 2/Hampshires in the centre and the 2/Coldstream on the left; fortunately this was later revised, leaving the two Guards' battalions on the Escaut and the Hampshires in reserve at Estaimbourg.

The 2/Coldstream arrived at Pecq at around 7.00pm on 19 May after an exhausting march of sixteen miles and were billeted in the École Moyenne along with the 2/Hampshires. The building remains almost exactly as it was in 1940 and is where the Coldstream Battalion HQ and

The school building remains much the same today as it was in May 1940.

the RAP were initially established. While most of the battalion got some sleep, two platoons from each company were detailed to begin digging rifle pits along their one mile frontage. The digging party used some colourful language! Please ensure that any photographs you take of the school do not contain any identifiable children.

> Continue to Estaimbourg and after passing the entrance to Château du Biez on your right continue round the left hand bend and park on the right near the church.

The village church at Estaimbourg. The churchyard cemetery can be seen on the right.

Estaimbourg was where the 2/Hampshires, under the command of Lieutenant Colonel Phillip Cadoux-Hudson, were placed in reserve. After marching from the École Moyenne, where they spent the night of 19 May, they linked up with Y Company, who had been billeted in Estaimbourg and formed a defensive ring around the village. It may be a sensible idea to leave your vehicle near the church and walk around the village, starting at the churchyard cemetery, where there are five casualties from the 1940 campaign. As you leave the churchyard, the continuation of the N510 which runs south-west towards the A17 Motorway, was the preserve of X Company. To your right, just past the war memorial, are the gates leading to Château de Bourgogne, where Lieutenant Colonel Cadoux-

Hudson established his HQ and where Brigadier Beckwith-Smith organized Brigade HQ. If you walk down the avenue leading to Château de Bourgogne and cross over the pedestrian foot bridge you will be in the area defended by Z Company. The battalion adjudant was delighted to find the château had extensive cellars:

> *The château had some really grand cellars and so made an ideal battle HQ. It was not long before the signallers were busy laying lines to HQ and within two hours we were ready for anything. Soon afterwards Jerry began shelling, and the noise made by exploding shells was terrific.*

The château is now a wedding venue and the author had little difficulty in asking to be shown round the interior of the building.

After returning to the entrance, gates the ground straight ahead of you, on the far side of the village square, is where Y Company guarded the approaches from the west, while to the north, W Company, with its HQ in Château du Biez, covered the approaches from the north. The Château du Biez is also a wedding venue and a stroll along the approach avenue

The Château de Bourgogne at Estaimbourg.

to view the building with its moat it well worth the effort. On returning to your vehicle, the author can recommend the Café la Cave de Bourgogne in the village square for a refreshment stop.

Lieutenant Colonel Bootle-Wilbraham moved the 2/Coldstream HQ on 20 May to what he calls 'an unnamed château on the road to Lille'. This château was more than likely the Château du Biez, particularly since the Hampshires and Beckwith-Smith had already commandeered Château de Bourgogne. The next day, when the German infantry of IR 12 crossed the Escaut at the junction of the two Guards' battalions, two companies of the Hampshires were moved out of the village in support of the Guards. Z Company, with one section from the Carrier Platoon, were detailed to move east down the Wasmes stream towards Plouy to meet them and Y Company were ordered into Pecq to support the Coldstream. Later, with the position on the Escaut stabilized, Z Company continued their move south to Bailleul and came under the command of the 3/Grenadier Guards.

> Retrace your steps to the crossroads at Pecq and continue straight ahead, past the Mairie for a further 270 yards, where you will see a turning on the right – Rue du Château. There is roadside parking here.

The Château Bernard at Pecq.

Walk down Rue du Château for seventy yards to where you can see a tree lined road leading to Château Bernard. This remarkable building was burnt down in 1450 and rebuilt only to be damaged again during the French Revolution. Surrounded by a moat, the two wings dating back to the 17th century still survive today. In May 1940 the surrounding land ran down to the edge of the Escaut where there was once a dock. This is where Lieutenant Colonel Phillip Cadoux-Hudson initially established the Hampshire's Battalion HQ, the Regimental historian describing it as:

> *An unusually luxurious château with valuable pictures and furniture, all deserted. There was a lake in the grounds and some enterprising spirits took out a rowing boat and fished with grenades and came back with a bucket full of small fish, a much appreciated addition to the irregular and Spartan fare of those bewildering days.*

Lieutenant Jimmy Langley of the Coldstream Guards also mentions the château in his account, recalling that it had a 'walled garden that ran down to the river bank'. They quickly came to the conclusion it would be a good defensive position and found:

> *A window in an upstairs bedroom overlooked not only most of 15 Platoon's area but also the ground in front of the company on our right flank. It did not take much military knowledge to realize that a machine gun, or two Bren guns, firing from the window would make any attack by day if not impossible, at least very hazardous.*

Walk back to the main road and turn right. Walk along the road for approximately sixty-five yards and stop opposite the large detached building.

In pre-war and wartime photographs this building features prominently as being the last building before the bridge crossed the Escaut. At the time of writing it goes under the name of the H2O-Club. The bridge, where Major Angus McCorquodale left orders with Sergeant Smith of the HQ Signals Platoon to shoot Lieutenant Jimmy Langley if he tried to sit or lie down, no longer exists, as during the post-war realignment of the Escaut the whole line of the river was moved 150 yards to the east and a new bridge constructed to cross the river. If you walk a few yards further along the road to where a large barn structure can be seen on the left, you are on the approximate site of the bridge that was here in May 1940. This is where Langley ordered the bridge to be blown at 1.00am

Jimmy Langley and Angus McCorquodale: a caricature by Gdsm. Kingshott, C Company

A cartoon drawn by Guardsman Kingshott in 1939 of Jimmy Langley and Angus McCorquodale.

on 20 May, an explosion that broke every pane of glass in the village and badly damaged the modern day H2O-Club premises. At daybreak a 'solid breastwork of *pavé* stones and bricks were built on the western approach to the ruined bridge'. Bootle-Wilbraham later wrote that the sapper officer on the bridge had persuaded Langley to order the demolition but, as Langley said afterwards, 'I was much too frightened of Angus's wrath if I blew the bridge too early without adequate reasons. I simply felt that under cover of the rising mist a determined attack had a high chance of success.'

> Turn around and drive back to the crossroads, where a right turn will take you back onto the N50. Continue for 350 yards and take the turning on the right – Bas Chemin – where you will see a disused factory complex on the left.

This is the site of the former tannery where No.4 Company was moved on 20 May. Bootle-Wilbraham writes that after reports that the building had been badly damaged by enemy shellfire he sent Captain Charles Blackwell up to investigate and take over command of the company if necessary. 'He arrived at Company HQ to find everyone hale, hearty and cheerful and rather enjoying the battle. The platoon in the tannery was having a first class shoot from the windows and claimed to have killed a number of Bosche.' Since May 1940 the building had had a chequered history and was at one time a poultry factory; today there is little to see and any fields of fire that existed in 1940 are now obscured by trees. But a short stroll around the outside of the deserted building will reveal the upper floor windows from where the men of No.4 Company opened fire on enemy troops and, presumably, from where Guardsman Swabey accounted for fourteen Germans with his rifle. It is only when you realize that the western bank of the river was considerably closer to the building than it is today that you understand why it was such a good vantage point.

The tannery in the Bas Chemin at Pecq.

Return to the crossroads and turn left to continue south along the N50 towards Pont-a-Chin for 0.66 miles until you see a crossroads. The turning on the right leads to Bailleul, where the 3/Grenadier Guards based their headquarters. We are going to take the left turning along a narrow road leading to Poplar Ridge.

It was from Bailleul that No.3 Company, under the command of Captain Lewis Starkey, and three carriers from Lieutenant Heber Reynell-Pack's Carrier Platoon moved across the N50 to counter-attack the German troops who had crossed the river at the junction of the Grenadier and Coldstream Guards. Under the watchful eye of Major Allan Adair, commanding the battalion, Starkey's orders were to link up with the Coldstream and push the Germans back across the river.

The *Chapel Notre Dame de la Misericorde* is 120 yards east of the N50

Poplar Ridge.

Les Drinkwater's barn, which was the 3rd Battalion Grenadier Guards' No.4 Company HQ. The double doors in the centre of the building have been replaced by a more functional glass threshold.

The narrow road you are on leads to a small junction by a private house. The modern day poplar plantation – Poplar Ridge – is behind you and this 'high ground' was the approximate area where Lance Corporal Harry Nicholls destroyed the momentum of the IR 12 assault and was subsequently awarded the VC. If you bear right at the junction for another 360 yards you will come to Esquelmes War Cemetery; take care here as the grass approach path on the left of the road is easy to miss and parking can be difficult.

After returning to your vehicle, continue to the T-junction and turn left. After 200 yards you will see a private house on the right. This is Les Drinkwater's barn (see Walk 1). Turn around and continue past the junction leading to Esquelmes War Cemetery until you reach another junction marked by a small shrine – *Chapel Notre Dame de la Misericorde* – where Captain Birch of the 2/North Staffordshires and a Grenadier corporal were rescued by Corporal Wade. Turn left and rejoin the N50. After 800 yards you will see a narrow turning on the right that leads to Esquelmes village and the churchyard cemetery. After returning to the N50 continue south past Pont-a-Chin to the Rue de l'Abbé Nestor Fère in Froyennes, north-west of Tournai.

The Château Beauregard at Froyennes.

The entrance to Château Beauregard is on Rue de l'Abbé Nestor Fère in Froyennes just opposite the pond. This is where Lieutenant Colonel Law established the 5/Border Regiment's HQ before moving a few miles south to La Marmite. Froyennes Communal Cemetery on Rue de Flequièries is a few minutes away, near the E42 Motorway. The tour concludes at Tournai Communal Cemetery, Allied Extension, on Chaussée de Willemeau, which is a fifteen minute drive using the Tournai Ring Road. You will find satellite navigation very useful for navigating in and around Tournai.

CEMETERIES
Helkijn Churchyard
The cemetery is located next to the church at the end of Kerkstraat and the five casualties are buried directly in front of the entrance. The 20-year-old **Guardsman Francis Sheppard** from Bristol, who was killed on 20 May, was serving with the 2/Grenadier Guards and is the only Second World War casualty.

Bailleul Communal Cemetery
The village of Bailleul is about one and a half miles west of the N50. The

Helkijn Churchyard Cemetery.

Bailleul Communal Cemetery.

cemetery is located on a small lane leading from the church and market square and the three Second World War graves are in the south-eastern corner. Buried here is **WO III (Platoon Sergeant Major) Frank Court** of the 2/Coldstream, who was a platoon commander with No.1 Company. He and his platoon remained in their positions on the river bank after IR 12 had affected a crossing to his right. He was killed sometime later on 21 May. Also here are 22-year-old **Guardsman Herbert Little,** 3/Grenadier Guards, and 21-year-old **Gunner Leonard Formston,** from

2/Field Regiment, Royal Artillery, who was killed on 19 May during counter-battery fire.

Estaimbourg Churchyard
The church is opposite the village square and contains six Second World War burials, one of which is unidentified. There are four gunner casualties from the artillery units supporting the 1st Division and **Private Walter Butlin** of the 2/Hampshires, whose death from shrapnel was remembered by the battalion's adjutant: 'A soldier was brought in from one of the forward companies. He had been wounded by shrapnel and died about two hours later. As there was a cemetery nearby, we decided to bury him there.'

Pecq Communal Cemetery
The cemetery is situated 600 yards north of the Pecq crossroads on the N50. There is a large parking area next to the entrance. The cemetery contains nineteen casualties from the Second World War, of whom two are unidentified. The two 1918 burials were both killed five days before the Armistice was declared on 11 November. Of the fourteen identified Coldstream Guards, the youngest is 18-year-old **Guardsman Hedley Knowles** from Skipton, who was killed on 21 May. Also here is **Captain Charles Fane,** the Coldstream Carrier Officer, who was killed on 21 May by a shell near Poplar Ridge; and buried nearby is 23-year-old **Lieutenant Hon Evelyn Boscawen**, who was killed on the night of 20 May and described by Lieutenant Colonel Bootle-Wilbraham as a serious loss to No.1 Company. 31-year-old **Captain John Trelawny**, a company commander with the 1/Suffolks, was killed by shellfire north of Pecq on 21 May at the same time as his commanding officer, Lieutenant Colonel Eric Frazer, who later died of his wounds. Trelawny's brother, Sergeant Gerald Trelawny RAFVR, was killed almost a year later in a flying accident.

Esquelmes War Cemetery
The cemetery is east of the N50 and can be accessed from the left hand turning 1.23 miles south of the Pecq crossroads. This will lead you to the shrine – *Chapel Notre Dame de la Misericorde* – where a right turn will take you to the junction with Trieu de la Savonnerie. Turn left here – signposted Esquelmes War Cemetery – and the cemetery is on the right. There are 201 identified casualties from the 1940 campaign buried here, of whom thirty-two are unidentified. Numbers swelled after the British had left the district, as many other casualties from surrounding areas were brought here to be re-interred, which accounts for the headstones of

twenty-five men of the Royal Warwicks who were fighting around Calonne and on the Ypres-Comines Canal in May 1940. Amongst the former is **Captain Timothy Mead,** who was spotting for 115/Field Regiment on 20 May near St Maur on the Escaut when his OP was hit by a shell. 21-year-old **Lieutenant Geoffrey Worke** of C Company, 1/6 Queen's, who was killed near Elsegem Château in the 44th Divisional area along with his Company Commander, **Captain Reginald Pontifex,** is buried alongside twenty-six of his battalion. Their number include **Lance Corporal W Benson** and **Private H E Benson,** two brothers who came from the Elephant and Castle district of London and 28-year-old **Captain Richard Rutherford,** commanding D Company, who was killed leading a counter-attack.

Of the thirty-three identified Grenadiers buried here, the most senior is **Captain Robert Abel-Smith,** who was killed with **Lieutenant The Duke of Northumberland** (Lt. Henry Percy) during the No.3 Company counter-attack on 21 May. Also buried here is **Second Lieutenant Arthur Boyd,** who was killed during No.4 Company's attempt to regain their lost positions and had only joined the battalion a few weeks previously. Interestingly, of the ten unidentified Grenadier Guard's casualties, one is

Esquelmes War Cemetery.

a Grenadier officer and there is a suggestion that this may be the grave of **Major Alston-Roberts-West,** who was seen to fall by Les Drinkwater on the banks of the Escaut. You will also find, amongst the six North Staffordshires' casualties, the grave of **Major Frederick Matthews,** who led the North Staffordshires' counter attack from Esquelmes on 21 May. Before you leave, find the headstone of **Private Anthony Wynne** of the 1/7 Royal Warwicks. Wynne was killed on the Ypres-Comines Canal at Houthem, where he single handedly held up any attempts by German infantry to cross the canal with sustained and accurate Bren gun fire. He was killed on 28 May by a shell and was originally buried in the dry canal bed before his body was reinterred here.

Templeuve Communal Cemetery
The cemetery is located at the end of the Rue Justin Bruyenne in Templeuve and contains thirteen casualties of the Second World War. Nearby are ten First World War graves from 1918. The seven men from 248/Field Company, Royal Engineers were all victims of shellfire, the war diary reporting a further forty men were injured, together with eleven vehicles and six motorcycles. **Pilot Officer Peter Bone** and his observer, **Sergeant William Cronin,** were both killed when their 53 Squadron Bristol Blenheim IV crashed near Foyennes on 15 May. Four days later, **Pilot Officer John Coleman** was shot down and killed flying a Photo Reconnaissance Spitfire; he had previously served with 19 Squadron.

Froyennes Communal Cemetery
Tucked away on the Rue de Flequières in Froyennes, this cemetery is a little difficult to find and satellite navigation is very useful. There are thirty-one casualties from the 1940 campaign buried here, six of whom are unidentified. The eleven identified men of the 1/Border Regiment, all killed on 21 May, underline the ferocious nature of the fighting that took place in the city along the river frontage. One of these was the 20-year-old **Second Lieutenant Desmond Fitzgerald**, a former Dulwich College schoolboy, who joined the regiment in July 1939. At the time of his death he commanded the carrier platoon and it is not unreasonable to presume some of his men are buried with him.

Tournai Communal Cemetery, Allied Extension
There is ample parking by this large cemetery, which can be found in the south-west quarter of the city on Chaussée de Willemeau. The CWGC plot is to the left of the main avenue and marked by the Cross of Sacrifice. Of the 699 identified casualties of both wars that are buried here, fifty-two are casualties from the fighting in May 1940, many of whom have

The entrance gates to Tournai Communal Cemetery.

been brought in from surrounding battlefields. One of these is 22-year-old **Second Lieutenant George Duncan,** of B Company, 1/Ox and Bucks Light Infantry, who was killed during the counter-attack at Hollain. Interestingly, there are 117 Russian burials, all of men who died as prisoners of war during the First World War. The thirteen men of the 1/6 Lancashire Fusiliers were part of the 125 Brigade counter-attack of 21 May in Tournai, some of whom would have died of wounds in the following days. It is likely that the five Border Regiment casualties, and those of the 1/East Lancashires, were also part of the defence of Tournai. Buried next to each other are the crew of a 59 Squadron Blenheim IV. 19-year-old **Pilot Officer Roy Durie** and his observer, **Sergeant Robert Burns**, both died on 18 May. 59 Squadron flew to France in October 1939 and operated throughout the 'phoney war' period and during the German offensive in May 1940. The squadron returned to England on 20 May.

Car Tour 4

Chercq to Warnaffles Farm

Start – Chercq Churchyard Cemetery
Finish – The track east of Warnaffles Farm
Distance – Ten miles

This tour begins at the churchyard cemetery at Chercq, which was defended by 4 Brigade, under the command of Brigadier Edward Warren, and gives you the opportunity to stretch your legs along the positions occupied by A Company of the 2/Royal Norfolks. We then move south through to Calonne and Hollain, from where we conclude the tour at Warnaffles Farm after looking at the route of the 8/Royal Warwicks counter-attack of 21 May.

> Chercq is best approached along the N502 from Tournai. After passing the prison in Tournai, it is about 1.2 miles to the church at Chercq on Rue de l'Eglise – which is on your right almost immediately after the war memorial. There is ample parking on the right hand side just before you reach the church.

We are now in the A Company sector of the 2/Royal Norfolks, whose Battalion HQ was at Château de Curgies on the outskirts of Calonne. A Company was commanded by Captain Peter Barclay, who had been awarded one of the first MCs of the war on the Maginot Line in January 1940. Continue uphill to the churchyard, where twenty-four Second World War casualties are buried. After leaving the church return to your vehicle and drive up hill past the church and follow the road round a right hand bend. After approximately 250 yards you will

The war memorial at Chercq.

Chercq Churchyard Cemetery on the Rue de l'Eglise.

The Château des Chartreux at Chercq.

come to the gates of Château des Chartreux, with a superb avenue of trees stretching away to your left. Stop here if you wish to take a photograph of the château building. This is the château referred to in Captain Peter Barclay's account of the battle, where he says he and his batman went hunting for rabbits in the grounds.

> *My batman reported that he'd seen some black rabbits in the park of a chateau in the grounds of which some of my* [Company's] *positions were. Not only that but he's found some ferrets and retrievers shut up in the stables. So I thought we'd get in a bit of sport before the fun began. I had a shotgun with me and we popped these ferrets down a big warren. We were having a rare bit of sport as rabbits bolted out of these burrows when, after about an hour-and–a–half, the shelling started along the river line generally.*

Interestingly, Private Ernie Leggett casts some doubt on the authenticity of this story, saying in his opinion it was not true, as the Germans were only 150 yards away and the Norfolks had more important things on which to focus their minds!

Continue for another 120 yards and turn right down Rue Haute, with the wall of the château grounds on your right. Follow the road downhill to the junction with the N502, where immediately across the road you will see a large parking area where you can leave your car. Here you will see a short track leading to the tow path running alongside the Escaut; once you are standing by the river, stop. The track which you have just used to reach the river was in the D Company sector, with C Company on their left further along the canal towards the disused railway bridge, which you can see in the distance. This is the beginning of a short walk along the tow path to the approximate position of Private Ernie Leggett's position and George Gristock's VC action.

As you walk along the tow path towards the road bridge you will move into the A Company sector. Barclay notes that the battalion took over positions from the 1/Royal Berkshires early on 20 May and at one point were in contact with D Company of the 1/8 Lancashire Fusiliers on their right:

> *These were on a fairly wide front, the battalion had a very long front to contend with and so, of course, my company front was also long, about 700 or 800 yards – which was a lot for a company in close country. There were buildings on our side of the canal and there was a plantation on the enemy side, so we had to have*

The modern day road bridge at Chercq.

> *a pretty effective system of cross fire ... I went round* [the company positions] *and they were jolly well camouflaged too. Some were in cellars with sort of loopholes under the roofs, one lot hiding behind a garden wall with loopholes – well concealed positions which gave good cover of the frontage I was responsible for.*

We will probably never have a completely accurate description of the Norfolks' positions along the Escaut, as listening to both Barclay's and Ernie Leggett's accounts one cannot help but identify a number of conflicting statements where perhaps the passage of time has eroded the accuracy of recall. Leggett in his account is quite adamant that the A Company front was little more than 120 yards long – although he may not have included the ground occupied by Barclay and the HQ Platoon. Even so, this is at odds with Barclay's estimation, in which he maintains the company occupied a front of some 800 yards. Leggett tells us he and his section were positioned in an old cement factory on the left flank of the A Company positions, from where he could look along to the right to where Barclay and the A Company HQ were positioned. It was from the cement factory that Leggett says he was able to watch CSM George Gristock attack the German machine gun posts.

Thus it would appear from these two accounts that the current road bridge is approximately in the position where the 'blitzed bridge' referred to by Barclay was situated. This would have been in the *centre* of HQ Platoon's positions, and not, as Barclay suggests, in the centre of A Company's positions. The area where CSM George Gristock's VC action occurred was to the right of the bridge, a notion which is supported by Ernie Leggett's account, in which he describes open ground between the cement factory and Gristock's attack on the German machine guns.

The post-war development of the location and the subsequent widening of the Escaut has substantially altered the landscape of the area and many of the features that are mentioned in the various accounts by officers and men of the Royal Norfolks have long been demolished. However, contemporary maps suggest that the widening of the river largely affected the eastern bank, and the western bank – on which you are standing now – is roughly in the same position as it was in May 1940.

After 600 yards you will pass the remains of former lime kilns – *Fours à Chaux*. These kilns were definitely in place in May 1940 and there is a useful information board with an English translation that provides a potted history of the building, which looks to have been more extensive in 1940. Whether or not this is Ernie Leggett's cement factory is open to conjecture. Walk on towards the bridge and stop at the next track on the right. Look immediately across the river to where you can

The remains of the *Fours à Chaux* lime kilns. Was this where Ernie Leggett was positioned?

The nineteenth century lime kiln south-east of the road bridge.

see a road to the right of the church leading down to the river, the Rue-des-Grinques. This is where the road bridge crossed in 1940; the bridge that you can see is the new bridge, which was positioned further east after the post-war reconstruction.

Quite where Captain Barclay was when he watched the Germans laying hurdles across the demolished bridge is unclear; but he says he was approximately a hundred yards away from the enemy as they crossed the Escaut and they 'were standing about in little groups, waiting'. The large square nineteenth century lime kiln on the far side of the bridge is a possible contender. But, wherever he was, the Norfolks must have been very well concealed, as when about twenty-five of the enemy had gathered on the western bank they were apparently totally oblivious of the presence of British troops:

> *I blew my hunting horn. Then of course all the soldiers opened fire with consummate accuracy and disposed of all the enemy personnel on our side of the canal and also the ones on the bank on the far side – which brought the hostile proceedings to an abrupt halt.*

Pass under the bridge, from where you will get a better view of the large nineteenth century lime kiln on the right. This was the junction between the 1/8 Lancashire Fusiliers and the Royal Norfolks, where the Germans got across the canal on 21 May and D Company of the Lancashire Fusiliers reported twenty-five per cent casualties.

Almost immediately after passing under the bridge, take the winding road on the right, which goes back to the main N502. Turn right again along the road on the pedestrian footpath towards the war memorial. In May 1940 this road was also the line of a local railway track that serviced the cement factories. The railway line crossed the road near the war memorial to run along the north-eastern edge of the grounds of Château des Chartreux before arriving at the former railway station. Once you pass the grounds of the château on your left, it is only 300 yards to where you parked your vehicle.

> As you leave Chercq by the N502 and pass Rue du Coulant d'Eau on the right – a cul de sac – the ground on your right begins to rise as you pass into the sector defended by the 1/7 Royal Warwicks. Continue until you reach reach Calonne Communal Cemetery on the right, where there is ample parking behind the war memorial.

If you stand by the war memorial, face the river and look across to your left; Château de Curgies, where the 2/Norfolks' Battalion HQ was based, is on the opposite side of the road. You can walk up to the entrance gates but a better view is to be had by walking down the track towards the river on the right of the building. This is where Major Nicholas Charlton, who

The former railway station at Chercq.

The Entrance to Calonne Communal Cemetery.

The Château de Curgies today.

had recently taken over command of the battalion, Major FR Marshall, the battalion's adjutant, and the Intelligence Officer, Second Lieutenant PS Buckingham, were all wounded on 21 May when a mortar shell landed in the château porch. Taking over command, 38-year-old Major Lisle Ryder had less than a week to live before he and the men of HQ Company were murdered by the SS at Le Paradis.

Before you continue into Calonne it is useful to have some understanding of Brigadier Muirhead's deployment of 143 Brigade's battalions. Brigade HQ was initially at Warnaffles Farm (on the D507) and from here Muirhead deployed the 1/7 Warwicks to the north of Calonne and the 8/Warwicks, under the command of Lieutenant Colonel Reginald Baker, in and to the south of Calonne. In reserve were the 1/Ox and Bucks (the 43rd Light Infantry as they preferred to be called) at St Maur, where Brigade HQ was moved on 20 May.

In the sector allotted to Reginald Baker's 8/Royal Warwicks, buildings were in evidence on both sides of the river, despite the ground rising steeply from the river. This was of little use to the defending Warwicks, as the mass of industrial buildings forced Baker to position three companies on the river line. C Company was on the right flank in touch with the 5/Gloucesters at Bruyelle, A Company covered the area in front of the Antoing Bridge – which was blown on 19 May – and B Company held Calonne. D Company were kept in reserve at Warnaffles Farm.

The 1/7 Warwicks, under Lieutenant Colonel Gerard Mole's command, held a front of some 1,000 yards, with two companies on the river front and two on the high ground to the north of Calonne, overlooking the river. On the battalion's left flank were the 1/8 Lancashire Fusiliers.

Mole established his HQ in an old brickworks somewhere on the high ground above Calonne Communal Cemetery, an area that was once heavily quarried. Although it is now redeveloped into the *Espace Vert des Cinq Rocs,* a huge quarry still lies beneath a cloak of trees and shrubs. Should you wish to take a walk, *Cinq Rocs* is less than half a mile away and can be reached by continuing on the N502 to the next junction, where a right turn will take you along Rue Émile Royer for 250 yards to a crossroads. Turn right into Chemin des Cinq Rocs and park. A short walk uphill will provide a panoramic view of the Escaut valley – though some of it is now masked by trees – and the view that Gerard Mole may have had from his HQ. However, it was a view that he did not have for long as the 1/7 Warwicks were relieved by the 1/Royal Scots during the night of 20 May – by which time the Germans were established in Calonne itself.

The view down towards the Escaut from the high ground above Calonne. In 1940 the view would not have been obscured by trees.

Lieutenant Colonel Harold Money, commanding the Royal Scots, was certainly unhappy with his new position which, as you can see, was on the forward slopes of a low hill and very exposed to mortar and shell fire – this was the high ground that saw the death of Major George Byam-Shaw, killed by shell fire. Unable to make contact with the beleaguered 8/Royal Warwicks on his right flank – who were desperately awaiting relief – Money deployed his men ready to receive the expected enemy attack. There is little point in looking at where he deployed his companies on the western bank of the river as post-war realignment has significantly altered its course. The thirty yard wide river and the buildings that lined its banks have long gone, as have the sweeping meanders that characterised the river below Chercq in 1940.

The Royal Scots' counter attacks on 21 May certainly checked the German advance across the river – eight carriers were lost in the fighting – and the Scots were reported to have reached a point some 300 yards from their objective before they were ordered to dig in. We know from the 4 Brigade war diary that Harold Money moved his battalion HQ back to Warnaffles Farm, where Reginald Baker had also established the 8/Royal Warwicks HQ. Contemporary sources suggest there were 'words spoken' between Money and Baker regarding the German presence in Calonne. Money is reported to have told Baker that he would have counter-attacked earlier had he been in Baker's position; a remark that clearly stung Baker into the disastrous action that ended with a huge loss of life on the slopes overlooking Calonne. Quite where Captain Neil Holdich was positioned when he witnessed Baker's counter-attack is unclear; but he must have been close to Warnaffles Farm at the time.

On returning to the crossroads with Rue Émile Royer, glance to the right where Chemin de Warnaf rises above Calonne. This is the track that Lieutenant Colonel Baker used during his counter-attack and takes you to Warnaffles Farm, which we will visit later. Continue into Calonne and stop in the large car park on the left.

The Chemin de Warnaf runs from the western edge of Calonne up to Warnaffles Farm.

It was somewhere along this road that Sergeant WH Bate and a party of eighteen men from B Company, 8/Royal Warwicks, were working their way up the road at dusk on 21 May when twelve German motorcyclists appeared coming towards them. Private James Gillespie – a former player with Luton Town Football Club – immediately opened fire from the hip with his Bren gun. Hitting the lead motorcyclist, the remainder ploughed into their unfortunate comrades and met the same fate. Bate's party all got back to Warnaffles Farm but, regrettably, Gillespie was killed a few days later.

Continue through Calonne. The road takes you past the bridge at Antoing, which was defended by Major Kenneth Hopkins and the men of A Company, 8/Royal Warwicks. As you drive south along the N502 you pass underneath the TGV railway line, which is just south of the approximate boundary between 143 Brigade and 144 Brigade, which was commanded by Brigadier 'Hammy' Hamilton. Drive through Bruyelle to the large roundabout on the N507 where you will see Bruyelle War Cemetery on the right. Follow the CWGC signposts for the cemetery and park.

The 144 Brigade HQ was at Wez-Velvain, with the 5/Gloucesters at Bruyelle, the 2/Royal Warwicks at Hollain and the 8/Worcesters in reserve at Brigade HQ. The Gloucesters were relieved by the 8/Worcesters on 21 May, who took over positions that were almost continually under fire from, what Second Lieutenant Bill Haywood described as, 'scattered parties of Germans on our side of the river'. There is a useful orientation map at Bruyelle War Cemetery depicting the Escaut as it was in 1940.

Continue along the N507 through Hollain until you see the church on your right. There is parking outside the church and in the immediate vicinity.

This is Hollain Churchyard Cemetery and the start of Walk 2, which takes you around the 2/Royal Warwicks positions in Hollain and looks at the ground over which the 1/Ox and Bucks counter-attacked on 21 May.

After leaving the church, turn around and take the first turning on the left – Rue de la Fontaine – and at the crossroads with Rue de Jollain go straight across and continue for 2.37 Miles to a T-junction. St Maur is to the left and the junction with the N507 is to the right, from where the entrance to Warnaffles Farm is immediately opposite. Turn right and then take the first road on the left – Chemin de Warnaf – marked by the large pylon standing in the field to the right. You can drive down here for a short distance to enable you to park, but take care not to block the road.

Warnaffles Farm is private property and permission is needed to go beyond the private house, but there is nothing left of the original buildings. This is where Reginald Baker established the 8/Royal Warwicks' HQ and at one point shared the accommodation with Harold

The entrance to the former Warnaffles Farm.

Money and the HQ of the 1/Royal Scots. Major Ralph Lowe was killed here standing in the porch of the farmhouse half an hour after he had taken over command of the 8th Battalion.

Of far greater interest is the Chemin de Warnaf, down which Lieutenant Colonel Baker and the men of the 8/Royal Warwicks HQ Company advanced during their ill fated counter-attack. Described as 'the only road leading west from Calonne' by the Royal Warwicks' regimental historian, Marcus Cuncliffe, it alternates today between a tarmac and gravel surface and, although the author has had little trouble negotiating the track in a 4x4, you may decide caution is the best approach and walk down towards Calonne. The track bears right, passing a tree encrusted former quarry on the left, before it begins to descend towards the western edge of Calonne. It is quite possible to imagine the V formation of officers and men from HQ Company with Baker in the lead using the line of the track. With him were the battalion's adjutant, Second Lieutenant Seymour Hewitt, the Signals Officer and Second Lieutenants Lawrence Strawson, Gordon Potts and Gerald Batten. As the German machine gunners opened up on the advancing Warwicks the ground on either side of the track would have become strewn with dead and dying men. According to Marcus Cuncliffe, only two men managed to return to Warnaffles Farm, one of whom was Private Charles Smirthwaite:

The track from Warnaffles Farm along which Lieutenant Colonel Baker counter-attacked the German infantry positions in the western edge of Calonne.

> We were confronted with light automatic fire. This grew more intense every second and the CO gave orders to get down and choose targets ... The enemy were well concealed, their fire coming from the direction of the houses in front. Our party opened fire, the main targets being the windows of a farmhouse. I heard our two Bren guns singing away their short life.

If you have decided to drive down the track, the tour concludes at Calonne; otherwise, retrace your steps and return to your vehicle near the farm.

CEMETERIES
Chercq Churchyard
The churchyard is located just off the main N502 on the Rue de l'Eglise. The twenty-four war graves of the Second World War are on the northern side of the church, close to the six graves of the First World War. Apart from **Private Dennis Sexton** of the 1/7 Royal Warwicks, the remaining six are all from the 8/Battalion, the most senior being 33-year-old **Major Ralph Lowe,** who was killed standing in the porch at Warnaffles Farm, having just taken over command of the battalion. The thirteen men of the Royal Norfolks and Lancashire Fusiliers were casualties from the defence of the canal around Chercq, as were **Second Lieutenant Leonard Anste**y and **Private William Clifford** of the 1/Royal Berkshires, who were relieved by the 2/Norfolks on 19 May.

Calonne Communal Cemetery

Approaching from Chercq the cemetery is on the right of the N502 just before Calonne is entered. All the seventy-one burials are 1940 casualties, four of whom remain unidentified. As you would expect, the men buried here are mostly casualties of the fighting that took place in and around Calonne. The forty-seven casualties from the Royal Warwickshire Regiment not only include 45-year-old **Lieutenant Colonel Reginald Baker** and many of the men who took part in the counter-attack from Warnaffles Farm, but also the two youngest casualties in the cemetery, **Second Lieutenant Gerald Batten** – the 8/Royal Warwicks Intelligence Officer – and **Private Frederick Huckett.** Both boys were 19-years-old when they were killed on 21 May. Also killed during Baker's counter-attack were **Second Lieutenant Seymour Hewitt**, the battalion adjutant, and **Second Lieutenant Gordon Potts**. Tragically, **Captain Guy Glover** was shot dead by one of his own corporals on 20 May, which was hardly a fitting end to his short career. 39-year-old **Captain Neil Robinson**, the medical officer

Second Lieutenant Gordon Potts, 8/Royal Warwicks.

Calonne Communal Cemetery.

attached to the 8/Royal Warwicks, was loading wounded into an ambulance when he was killed by shellfire. The majority of the twelve casualties from the 1/Cameron Highlanders were probably victims of the battalion's counter-attack on the Bois de Lannoy on 21 May. 29-year-old **Private Duncan Johnstone** from 12 Platoon was killed serving in B Company, along with Privates Galloway and Johnstone, who are buried at Bryuelle War Cemetery.

Bruyelle War Cemetery

The cemetery is located at the junction of the N507 and N52. This is one of the largest cemeteries in the area and contains 146 casualties – seventeen of whom are unidentified – from the fighting in 1940. **Major Kilner Swettenham** remains the only casualty from the Allied advance in 1944 to be buried here. In November 1940 several casualties were brought in from the surrounding battlefields, which accounts for **Major George Byam-Shaw** and the twelve men of the 1/Royal Scots who were killed fighting near Calonne. Apart from **Private Arthur Matthews** of the 1/Suffolks, the remaining casualties are largely representative of those units that fought in the sector. Killed by a shell, 19-year-old **Lance Bombardier Thomas Bennett**, from 140/Field Regiment, Royal Artillery, was originally buried at St Maur, close to where his battery was operating. His grave was tended during the war years by a local English woman until he was reinterred at Bruyelle. **Captain Michael Potts**, from 68/Field Regiment, Royal Artillery, was killed while acting as a Forward Observation Officer at Bruyelle; his older brother, Second Lieutenant Gordon Potts, who is buried at Calonne Communal Cemetery, was killed on the same day. Another FOO, **Lieutenant Arthur Van Someren,** from 18/Field Regiment, was killed in his observation post on 20 May. Several

Bruyelle War Cemetery.

of the 1/Cameron Highlanders from B Company, who were killed during the battalion's counter-attack on the Bois de Lannoy on 21 May, are also buried here. **Lance Corporal Daniel Galloway,** from 12 Platoon, was killed alongside **Private Robin Johnstone** and **Private Willian Rae,** hit by the same shell that killed Second Lieutenant Peter Grant (commemorated on the Dunkirk Memorial). There are also nine casualties from the 1/Ox and Bucks Light Infantry, many of whom were killed during their counter-attack on the Bois de Lannoy, two of these being **Second Lieutenant Phillip Ingham** and **Sergeant Roland Wicks,** who died together as the battalion advanced out of Lesdain. Three men serve to remind us of the sacrifice made by the Royal Air Force during the campaign; 21-year-old **Pilot Officer Chris Mackworth,** from 87 Squadron, baled out of his Hurricane but was killed after his parachute caught fire. He was one of four pilots from 87 Squadron shot down on 14 May. **Corporal Reginald Tamblin** and **Pilot Officer Peter Peace** from the St Omer based 4 Squadron were both killed when their Westland Lysander crashed at Bruyelle.

Hollain Churchyard
The Churchyard is located in the village of Hollain and the CWGC plot can be found in the south-east corner. There are forty-one Second World War burials here, of whom over half are men of the 2/Royal Warwicks; sadly, seven of them are unidentified. 21-year-old **Second Lieutenant Kenneth Hope-Jones**, who was killed on 21 May, found himself commanding D Company after the death of **Major Phillip Morley,** who was killed trying to silence an enemy machine gun post. He apparently got to within fifteen yards of the post when he was shot down and the grenade he was holding exploded in his hand. Both officers died alongside their men, many of whom lie in the same churchyard. **Second Lieutenant Michael Gammidge** was two years older than Hope-Jones and died of wounds received while commanding his platoon in C Company during the afternoon of 21 May. The six men from the 1/Ox and Bucks light Infantry were probably casualties of the battalion's counter-attack on 21 May. **Sergeant Arthur Cruickshanks,** who commanded the 2/Royal Warwicks' Mortar Platoon, was accidentally shot and killed by one of his own men in a tragic mistake over passwords.

Walk 1

Pecq and Poplar Ridge

A circular walk, starting and finishing at Rue de la Croix Rouge
Distance: Three miles
Grade: Easy

This is a gentle stroll that looks more closely at the Coldstream and Grenadier positions and visits Esquelmes War Cemetery and Poplar Ridge on the way. From the Mairie in Pecq continue along the road towards the road bridge and park in Rue de la Croix Rouge, which is almost opposite Rue de Château. Walk along the road towards the bridge, noting the large barn like structure on your left, which was the approximate position of the bridge before the Escaut was realigned. This is the site of the bridge which was blown at 1.00am on 20 May and where Major Angus McCorquodale left orders with Sergeant Smith of the HQ Signals Platoon to shoot Lieutenant Jimmy Langley if he tried to sit or lie down! Continue to the modern day road bridge ❶ and, using the steps on the right, descend to the tow path below. The first thing to bear in mind is that in

The new bridge at Pecq.

Map labels:
- N 510
- Pecq
- Ecole Moyenne
- Estaimbourg
- Coldstream Guards
- Grenadier Guards
- Bailleul
- Chapel Notre Dame
- North Staffordshires
- Esquelmes
- N 50
- N (compass)

Walk 1
Pecq and Poplar Ridge

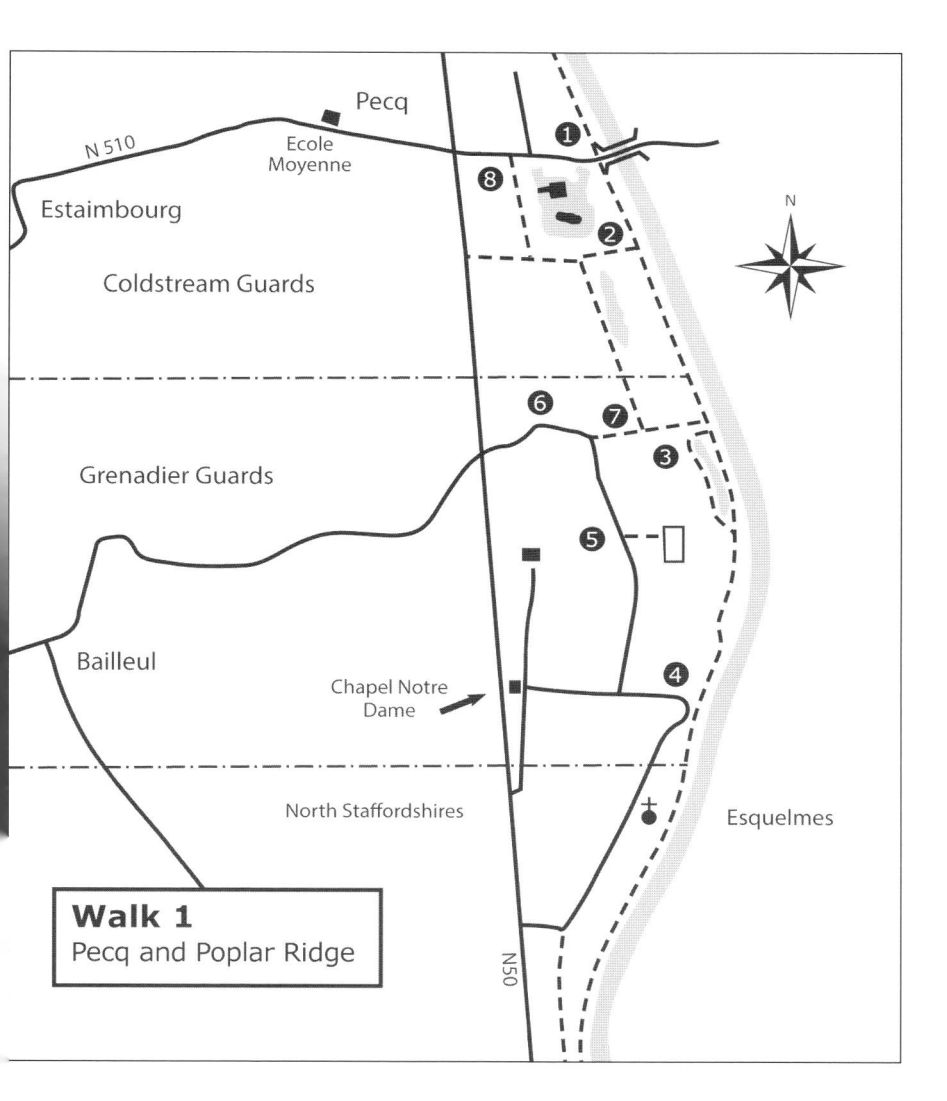

reality you are now on what was the eastern bank of the Escaut as it was in 1940! The British positions were 150 yards across to your right beyond the screen of trees. However, with this in mind, continue along the tow path, from where you might just get a glimpse of Château Bernard ❷ on your right which is almost hidden from view by the vegetation.

Jimmy Langley's 15 Platoon were positioned along the canal bank in front of the château and, apart from utilizing the bedroom windows of the building as a vantage point for two of his platoon's Bren guns, he recalls an incident in which a voice shouted for help from across the far side of the river. 'Hi! Can any of you fellows over there swim? I am not very good at it and I have a wounded man with me.' Had he but known it, the 'voice' was a German soldier and a trap was about to be sprung:

> *If the Germans had waited three seconds more before opening fire I think they would have wiped out the platoon. As it was they fired as soon as the first three men had climbed out of the slit trenches onto the top of the bank, killing one and wounding the other two, but warning all the rest of the trap ... To describe 15 Platoon as disorganized would be an understatement. If they had scrambled out of the trenches up the bank fast, without, of course, their rifles, it was nothing to the speed with which they tumbled back, momentarily shocked and unnerved.*

Later that day Captain John Pigott-Brown was wounded by a sniper's bullet in the 15 Platoon sector.

As you walk down the side of the river, glance across to the left to the high ground of Mont St Aubert. It was from the church tower at the top that the Germans were able to observe almost every move made by the British along the river. After 400 yards you will pass a turning on the right; ignore this and continue straight ahead to the next turning on the right –Trien de la Savonnerie. Turn right here and then, after sixty yards, turn left.

The high ground of Mont St Aubert overlooked the whole divisional front.

You are now going to walk alongside a 500 yard section of the old Escaut ❸ that would have been part of the river line in May 1940. This was the approximate junction between No.1 Company of the 2/Coldstream on the left and the 3/Grenadier Guards on the right, with No.4 Company occupying the ground ahead of you along the river to where Major 'Reggie' Alston-Roberts-West had established his HQ in a large barn close to the bank. It was in this area that Lieutenant Hon Evelyn Boscawen, from the Coldstream No.1 Company, was killed while on his way to Company HQ during the night of 20 May.

The two battalions of IR 12 launched their attack from Leaucourt at 7.30am on 21 May at the junction of the two Guards' battalions. Their preparations on the far side of the river had been shrouded by the early morning mist and the screen of riverside vegetation and the first thing the Grenadiers knew of the attack was a violent mortar and machine gun barrage along the whole width of the brigade sector. Described as 'slightly wider than the Basingstoke Canal', the Germans were soon across the river and through the forward posts of No.4 Company.

The two counter-attacks which followed only involved the Grenadier Guards. The first was by No.4 Company, whose left flank had taken a tremendous battering. Led by Major Alston-Roberts-West, he and one of the platoon commanders, Second Lieutenant Arthur Boyd, were killed in the unsuccessful attempt to regain their lost positions. Guardsman Les Drinkwater remembered Major Alston-Roberts-West 'running along the river bank towards us, exposing himself to enemy fire. When I looked up again he had disappeared.' The second counter-attack involved one platoon from No.1 Company and a few men from Nos. 2 and 4 Companies led by Captain Peter Radford-Norcop. This attack succeeded in establishing a position behind No.4 Company's old trenches. But it was costly. Only a handful survived and the German assault had not been halted.

Continue on down the towpath until you are able to access the path on your left through some bollards. The building immediately ahead of you is where No.4 Company HQ ❹ was situated and where Guardsman Les Drinkwater and the wounded Arthur Rice escaped after a clash with German infantry:

> *I found a stretcher and blankets for Arthur Rice and a nice pile of straw for myself, where I laid completely exhausted. The shelling had stopped, bullets were ricocheting off the roof and walls of the barn ... The enemy were closing in – drastic action had to be taken to enable us to escape.*

The barn which housed the 3rd Grenadiers No.4 Company HQ and the scene of Les Drinkwater's escape.

The barn has now been converted into a private house; but if you walk round to the front of the building, you can still see where the double doors faced the river and opened out towards the road. The breakout was more akin to a Boy's Own adventure story:

> *Two senior NCOs set up a Bren gun outside the large double doors – once they had started firing we had to start the vehicle motors (the noise of the Bren would deaden the sound of motors starting). The stretcher with Arthur lay diagonally across the vehicle, except for the driver's position, there was no cover at all – apart from the tail and side boards. I crouched alongside the stretcher, my rifle at the ready. We were fortunate the doors faced the bank – the enemy were closing in from the rear. A decision had been made for the first truck to turn left and the other to the right ... On clearing the barn we ran straight into the enemy – the essence of surprise was with us. At this stage the enemy dared not fire at us in case they hit each other; once we were through, a hail of bullets hit the truck, wounding our driver, but we continued and were soon over a ridge of high ground and out of sight of the enemy.*

We are now going to visit Esquelmes War Cemetery. Turn right in the direction of the N50 and walk along the road to the next junction. Turn right here along Trieu de la Savonnerie until you reach the grass approach path on the right leading down to the cemetery. ❺

On leaving the cemetery turn right and continue for another 200 yards and stop. This is a good point to view the counter-attack made by the Grenadier's No.3 Company, who had been called up from Bailleul by Major Adair. Captain Lewis Starkey formed his men up along the line of the N50 and began to advance under cover of a smoke screen. With support from Lieutenant Heber Reynell-Pack's carriers and the Grenadier Mortar Platoon, all went remarkably well until the mortars stopped firing under the mistaken belief that any further bombardment would hit Starkey's men. German machine gunners wasted no time in exploiting this 'gap' in the Grenadier's advance and brought Starkey's advance to a temporary halt. But Starkey had pinpointed the two machine gun posts that were causing all the trouble; one was near the river bank amongst the old No.4 Company trenches – which were across to your right – and the other was on a ridge of high ground ❻ crowned by a line of Poplar trees. There *Hauptmann* Lothar Ambrosius and about seventy men of IR 12 were dug in on what had become known as Poplar Ridge, which in 1940 ran along a different axis – north-west to south east. From where you are standing you can see this line of Poplar trees across to the left,

The approach path to Esquelmes War Cemetery. In the background the trees mark the line of the Escaut.

The high ground of Poplar Ridge where Lance Corporal Harry Nicholls won his Victoria Cross.

The Poplar plantation that existed in 1940 has long been replaced but still crowns the high ground.

beyond the electricity pylons. The current Poplar plantation is considerably younger than those trees that were in existence in May 1940, but a closer inspection will reveal a number of tree stumps that may well be the remnants of the trees that stood on the high ground in 1940.

Dividing his company into two parties, the right hand group, led by Captain Robert Abel Smith, charged the old No.4 Company positions along a line almost directly in front of you, while the left hand party, under Lewis Starkey, moved forward to the high ground. Captain Abel Smith's men were cut down, along with Lieutenant the Duke of Northumberland, before they reached the river bank, leaving the survivors isolated and in great danger from the German machine guns on Poplar Ridge. Reynell-Pack's carriers charged the German gunners on the high ground almost head on, but the rough ground worked against the Bren gunners, who were unable to bring any weight of fire down on the German positions. Reynell-Pack was killed in the leading carrier and the remaining two vehicles were forced to retire.

Starkey's men were in a desperate situation. Guardsman Percy Nash remembered being unable to proceed as the casualties mounted and the number of men dwindled rapidly. It was at that moment that Lance Corporal Harry Nicholls ran forward, with Nash supplying him with Bren gun magazines. On the Poplar Ridge *Hauptmann* Ambrosius recalled the alarm that the attack caused amongst his men as Nicholls silenced first one and then another machine gun and their crews:

> *The attack caused panic amongst the soldiers of our 5 and 6 Kompanies, many of whom fled and jumped into the Schelde* [Escaut] *to escape.* Oberleutnant *Shrumpel and* Leutnant *Schlinke then rallied these men who held their position on the river bank.* Leutnant *Engel, the Adjutant, was killed, shot through the head just a metre from me. It was he, with his fresh daredevil personality, who had led the Kompanies forward.*

Nicholls' gallant action not only enabled Captain Radford-Norcap's men, who had been pinned down by the machine guns on Poplar Ridge, to move forward but also – more crucially – checked the German advance. The Germans may have rallied on the river bank but their anticipated move on Bailleul had been stopped. Not only that but the arrival of A Company of the North Staffordshires from Esquelmes may well have tipped the balance of success in favour of the British. *Hauptmann* Ambrosius and the surviving men of IR 12 finally withdrew across the river.

Continue to the next junction and turn right by the single private house. You are now heading back towards the river, passing another remnant of the old Escaut surrounded by trees to your right. About 130 yards further along the track – just before you reach the river bank – you will see a wide grass pathway ❼ on the left. Take this path and keep the line of trees on your right to reach a junction after some 480 yards. Turn left at the junction for 250 yards until the track swings round to the right and leads straight on to Rue de Château. En-route you will be walking around two sides of the grounds of Château Bernard, which you may get a glimpse of through the trees. Failing that, the tree-lined entrance avenue is sixty-five yards from the junction of Rue de Château with the main road. Although this is private property, the author has not encountered any difficulty in taking photographs of the entrance gates. Continue to the main road ❽ and your vehicle.

The Château Bernard can be glimpsed through the trees.

Walk 2

Hollain

A circular walk starting and finishing at Hollain Church
Distance: Two miles
Grade: Easy

This short walk came about after reading the private diary of Captain Dick Tomes, who was the Adjutant of the 2/Royal Warwicks during the 1940 campaign, and follows a journey he made on several occasions when visiting the various company positions while the battalion was in Hollain. We also look at the ground over which three companies of the 1/Ox and Bucks counter-attacked the wooded area around Château de Lannoy.

Before we begin it may be useful to remind ourselves of the 2/Royal Warwicks' deployment at Hollain. Dick Tomes describes the river as some thirty yards wide and heavily built up on the western side, although on the 'enemy bank' the ground was comparatively open. Hollain itself lay partially on rising ground and back from the river. The weak point in the battalion's frontage – 2,800 yards according to Tomes – lay opposite D Company on the left flank, where a meander in the line of the river offered good cover for any attempt to cross it. It should also be remembered that the river was considerably closer to the village in May 1940 than it is now. A Company was on the right of D Company and B and C Companies were deployed on the right flank. Consequently, each of the four rifle companies had a front of approximately 700 yards and were positioned right up to the river bank in order to have effective fields of fire. Tomes also noted that the battalion's right flank was open at the junction with 145 Brigade. Battalion HQ is described as being 'set up in a house down a side street in the village'. From Tomes' description it would appear this was somewhere north of the church.

The walk begins at the Church, ❶ close to where Lieutenant Colonel Dunn had deployed the mortar section, which was originally under the command of Sergeant Arthur Cruickshanks, but now in the capable hands of Sergeant Brown. Tomes writes that just before dusk on 20 May he was given the task of taking a message to the mortar section with instructions for them to open fire on a group of German infantry grouping together on the far side of the river. The journey was not an easy one as the German artillery was shelling the village and almost every house appeared to have been hit and brickwork was flying in every direction:

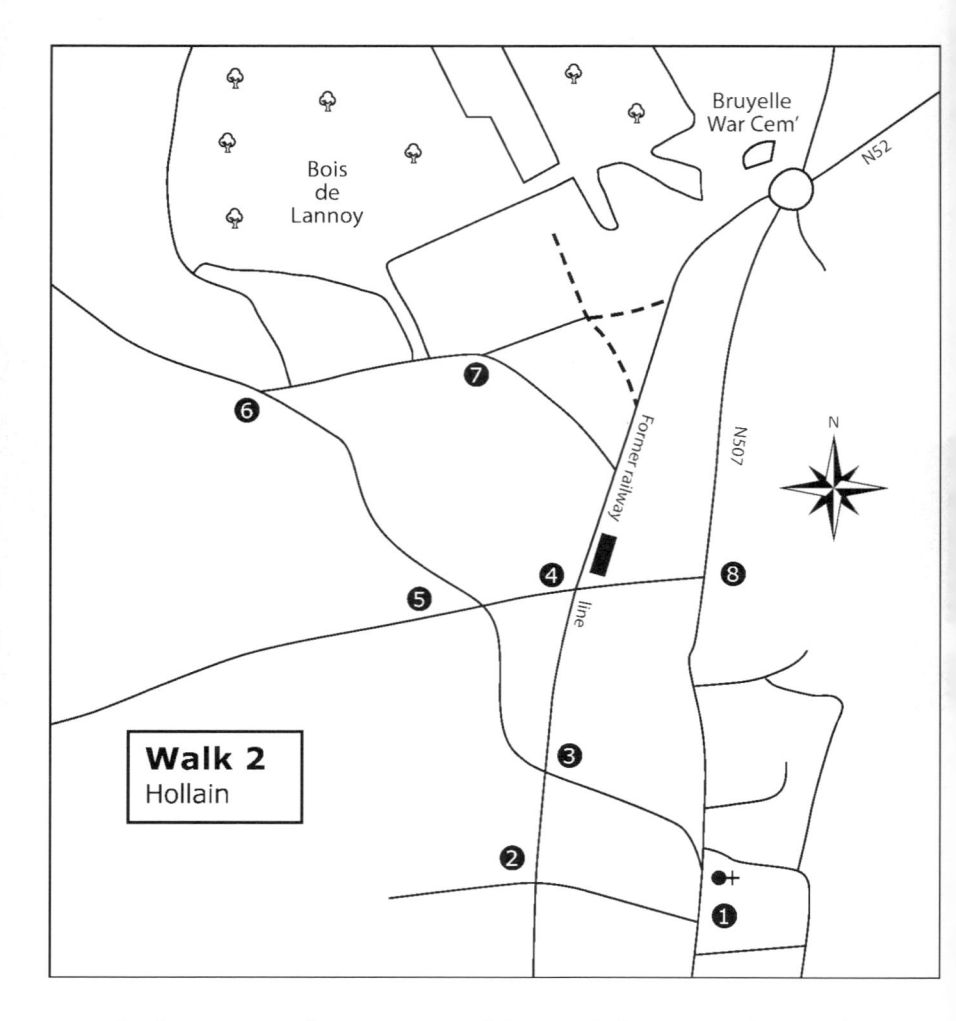

> *I ran hard to the churchyard and then it seemed to me that I was chased by bursting shells all round the church. I worked my way round the buttresses trying to get to the right side. Twice, just as I had got round a buttress, a piece of shell landed where I had been a moment before. I felt too keyed up and busy trying to get*

The church at Hollain. The CWGC plot is further to the right.

out of the way of falling debris to be frightened ... I eventually reached a point near the wall I should have to climb and dashed across the graveyard. It took me what seemed like hours climbing the wall and to get through a shrubbery before I reached the shelter of a slit trench where the mortar section was. Sgt Brown, who was in charge, came over from another trench and I showed him his target on the map ... I stayed until the mortars opened fire and until the German shelling had died down and then returned to Bn. HQ at speed, getting thoroughly tied up in fallen telegraph wires on the way back.

The next day, Tomes writes, he and Sergeant Underhay discovered Cruickshank's body in an archway opposite the church. 'Underhay was rather shaken for they had apparently been great friends.'

Keeping the church on your left, walk down the main street for approximately eighty yards before turning right into Rue Cazier. In just over a hundred yards further on you will see a narrow pathway on your right, ❷ which is where the former railway line ran and was used by Tomes on several occasions when avoiding the main street. Turn right and follow this pathway to the junction with the Rue de la Fontaine. ❸ Battalion HQ was probably somewhere amongst these private houses; we do know that the building had a fairly extensive cellar where the pioneers knocked a hole into the next door cellar in order to accommodate the signal exchange.

Cross straight over Rue de la Fontaine and continue along the track for another 300 yards until you reach the junction with Rue de Jollain. ❹ The track continues towards Bois de Lannoy, which you can see in the distance, and passes the former railway station building on the right. D Company HQ was further along the track, near the edge of the wood. On 20 May Dick Tomes wrote:

> *Everything calmed down at dusk and, except for spasmodic bursts of fire, nothing happened. I had some supper and then volunteered to take some stragglers of D Company along to their company and at the same time to visit* [Major] *Phillip Morley's*

The former railway station at Hollain and the track leading up to the Bois de Lannoy.

HQ. I had not been there before but thought I could find the way as it was a moonlight [sic] night and I knew the approximate position. We made our way along the railway line and through A Company's posts. *I came across* [Second Lieutenant] *Goodliffe and a few men in a patch of corn in the middle of a field – he had been waiting there for some time to try to attract the attention of the nearest post, which, he said, did not know he was out and would fire on him if he crossed that particular piece of field. ... It was pointless waiting there so I took the lot across and trusted to good luck that we would be challenged, as we were. I found Phillip in his Company HQ – a serviceable ditch at the edge of a big wood, handed him his men, gave him the latest news of the situation, got a drink of rum out of CSM Jennings and started back. That was the last I saw of Phillip, as he was killed the next day. On the way back I stopped to talk to L/Cpl Green's section on the railway line and then walked round* [Second Lieutenant] *Percy Chapman's platoon posts, as he was visiting them and met me.*

For the moment we are going to leave the 2/Royal Warwicks and turn left to walk along Rue de Jollain, which was the start line used by B and C Companies of the 1/Ox and Bucks Light Infantry on the 21 May attack on Bois de Lannoy. Tempers were already a little frayed, as on the previous day the battalion was told to proceed under the orders of 145 Brigade to Lesdain, from where they were to launch a counter-attack on Hollain with the 2/Gloucesters. This attack was cancelled at the last minute after the Warwicks managed to contain the Germans and were in the process of routing them out of the riverside buildings. But any thought of rest and recovery was out of the question for Lieutenant Colonel Whitfeld's men when orders for an immediate counter-attack on German infantry in Bois de Lannoy arrived, this time from 144 Brigade:

> *Two companies were to clear the wood of Germans and one company to fight its way through the western edge of Hollain and then northwards, with its right on the railway to form a defensive flank facing east about the bend in the railway ... Divisional artillery was to fire concentrations on the Bois de Lannoy until 1.30pm.*

Continue along Rue de Jollain to the next ❺ right hand turning – Rue du Grintier – and stop. If you turn and face north, looking towards Bois de Lannoy, you are probably standing close to where Lieutenant Colonel

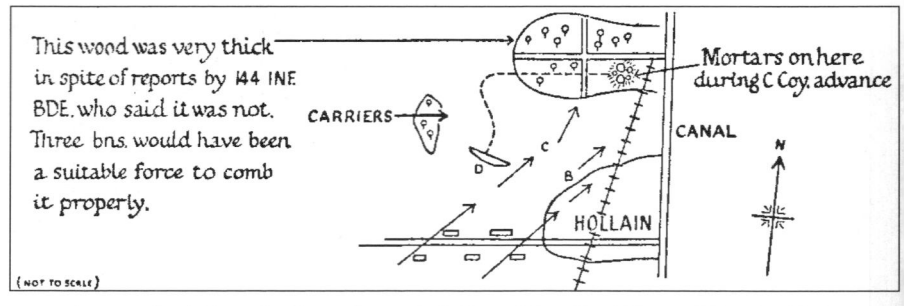

> This wood was very thick in spite of reports by 144 INF. BDE. who said it was not. CARRIERS
> Three bns. would have been a suitable force to comb it properly.
>
> Mortars on here during C Coy. advance
> CANAL
> HOLLAIN
> (NOT TO SCALE)

A map depicting the line of attack followed by the 1/Ox and Bucks Light Infantry on 21 May. Taken from Lieutenant Colonel Whitfield's account of May 1940.

'Whitters' Whitfeld established his battalion HQ. B Company, with its right flank on the railway, was advancing towards the bend in the railway – which was near to Bruyelle War Cemetery – and C Company was moving diagonally across the open ground in front of you towards the south face of the wood. Across to the left, D Company was advancing from the west, intending to cover C Company's advance into the wood before entering the wood themselves. In addition, the carriers, advancing from a small copse to the north-west – which is no longer in existence – would lay down heavy Bren gun fire on the wood. As one officer later remarked, 'it closely resembled a pheasant shoot'.

Now walk up Rue du Grintier, past the shrine on the right, to where the view opens up south of Bois de Lannoy. The ground over which C Company advanced is in front of you and by 2.25pm they had entered the wood relatively unopposed. As they were seen disappearing into the depths of the wood, Lieutenant Colonel Whitfeld noted with some surprise that [B Company] the 1/Cameron Highlanders were spotted attacking the wood from the direction of Merlin. Whether Brigadier Muirhead, commanding 143 Brigade, had prior knowledge of this attack is uncertain, as the Highlanders were a 2nd Division battalion. But the Cameron Highlanders eventually linked up with D Company of the 1/Ox and Bucks, passing through the wood either side of Château de Lannoy. Reading the account written by Captain Ronald Leah, commanding the Cameron Highlanders' B Company, it appears that they suffered heavily in the attack.

After another 250 yards take the track on the right ❻ that heads west and parallel to Bois de Lannoy. C Company would have advanced from

The Château de Lannoy as it is today.

The Western Avenue in the Bois de Lannoy, along which elements of B Company, 1/Cameron Highlanders may have advanced on 21 May.

Rue de Jollain, which you can see on your right, over the ground you are on to enter the southern edge of the wood. Continue along the track through a line of trees to where there is another indistinct path ❼ on the left. If the weather is good this path will take you directly to the former railway line near to where Major Phillip Morley established the 2/Royal Warwicks' D Company HQ. However, in wet weather this path does become very muddy.

We are going to continue along the track, which now swings round to the right to run parallel with the former railway line 250 yards further to the south-east. As you walk down the track you will shortly come to the former railway station building and Rue de Jollain. Tomes' diary account notes that: 'A few men with LMGs had succeeded in gaining a foothold on our side and were shooting from gardens in front of A Company'. However, by the time darkness fell the battalion was still holding onto its positions. What he does not say is that the Warwicks spent some time locating the enemy in a rigorous house-to-house search. Second Lieutenant Bill Haywood, the 144 Brigade Intelligence Officer, joined a patrol of the Warwicks who were hunting down these German infiltrators:

> *A Bren gun sprayed the windows and, under cover of its fire, two burly men rushed across the street and hurled themselves at the door. This gave way with a loud cracking noise, and the two men dashed in and straight up the stairs. I could see one stumble against a chair near the door, but he did not stop. The Bren fired another long burst, while the rest of us scampered over the road and through the open door. Four men searched the rooms downstairs without orders, while the subaltern and the remainder ran upstairs. I ran behind, eager to help but anxious not to get in the way. The subaltern was very cool. He knew which room to attack, since only one looked out over the street ... One of the two men, already at the top of the stairs, went forward and kicked in the door, while the other tossed a grenade inside. We all threw ourselves down for a moment, jumped up and dashed inside ... A German lying almost on his back fired a sub-machine gun, but the bullets sprayed the walls above our heads. One man threw himself on this German, who screamed with agony. The wretched fellow had been badly wounded by the grenade, and the impact of our man's knee made the blood gush from his stomach. The other two Germans were dead already.*

The main street near the church at Hollain before the war. The town was almost completely demolished by German artillery in May 1940.

Turn left at the junction with Rue de Jollain ❹ and walk along to the N507 where a right turn will take you along the main street of Hollain, which was badly damaged by German shellfire. Tomes writes of the 'telegraph wires' that were strewn across the street and caused untold problems in the darkness, badly cutting the face of Sergeant Jones 'who did great work on his motor bike taking messages to Brigade HQ'. Continue along the footpath to the church ❶ and your vehicle.

Appendix

Order of Battle – Escaut 1940
Commander-in-Chief – General The Viscount Gort VC

GHQ Troops

Armoured	Infantry	Royal Artillery	Royal Engineers
12/Royal Lancers 4/7 Royal Dragoon Guards 5/Royal Inniskilling Dragoon Guards 13/18 Royal Hussars 15/19 The Kings Royal Hussars **1/Light Armoured Reconnaissance Brigade** 1/Fife and Forfar Yeomanry 1/East Riding Yeomanry **2/Light Armoured Reconnaissance Brigade** 1/Army Tank Brigade 4 and 7/Battalions Royal Tank Regiment	1/Welsh Guards 7/Cheshires 1/8 Middlesex 4/Gordon Highlanders 6/Argyll & Sutherland Highlanders **Pioneers:** 6,7,8,9/Kings Own Royal Regiment 1/6 South Staffordshire 9/West Yorkshires	1,39/Army Field Regiments; 1,2,4,58,61,63,65,69 Medium Regiments 1,51,52 Heavy Regiments 1,2,3 Super Heavy Batteries 1/Anti-Aircraft Brigade: 1,6,85 Anti-Aircraft Regiments 2/Anti-Aircraft Brigade: 60 Anti-Aircraft Regiment 4/Anti-Aircraft Brigade: 4/Anti-Aircraft Regiment, 1/Light Anti-Aircraft Regiment 5/Searchlight Brigade: 1,2,3/Searchlight Regiments	100, 101, 216/Army Field Companies 228, 242/Field Companies 223/Field Park Company 19/Army Field Survey 58,61,62/Chemical Warfare Companies

I Corps
GOC: Lieutenant General Michael George Barker

Corps Troops

Royal Artillery	Royal Engineers	Infantry	
27, 140/Field Regiments 3, 5/Medium Regiments 52, 2/Light Anti--Aircraft Regiment 1/Survey Regiment	102, 140, 221/Field Companies 105/Field Park Company 13/Corps Field Survey Company	2/Cheshires 4/Cheshires 2/Manchesters	

2nd Division (With Rustyforce from 24-26 May and III Corps from 26 May)
GOC: Major General Henry Charles Lloyd until 16 May, Brigadier General Francis Henry Davidson 16-20 May, Major General Noel Mackintosh Irwin from 20 May.

4 Brigade	5 Brigade	6 Brigade	Artillery
GOC: *Brig Edward Warren* 1/Royal Scots 2/Royal Norfolks 1/8 Lancashire Fusiliers	GOC: *Brig Gerald Gartlan* 2/Dorsetshire 1/ Cameron Highlanders 7/Worcestershires	GOC: *Brig Noel Irwin* and *Brig Dennis Walter Furlong* (after 20 May) 1/Royal Welch Fusiliers 1/Royal Berkshire 2/Durham light Infantry	10, 16, 99/Field Regiments 13/Anti-Tank Regiment **Royal Engineers** 5, 209, 99 Field Companies 21/Field Park Company

42nd (East Lancashire) Division (With I Corps from 19 May)
GOC: Major General W G Holmes

125 Brigade	126 Brigade	127 Brigade	Artillery
GOC: *Brig GW Sutton* 1/ Border Regiment 1/5th Lancashire Fusiliers 1/6th Lancashire Fusiliers	GOC: *Brig E G Miles* 1/ East Lancashire 5/ King's Own Royal 5/ Border Regiment	GOC: *Brig J G Smyth* 1/ Highland Infantry 4/ East Lancashire 5/ Manchesters	52, 53/Field Regiments 56/Anti-Tank Regiment **Royal Engineers** 200, 201, 250/Field Companies 208/Field Park Company

48th (South Midland) Division
GOC: Major General Augustus Francis Thorne (Andrew)
(Under the command of GHQ from 25 May)

143 Brigade	144 Brigade	145 Brigade	Artillery
GOC: *Brig J Muirhead*	GOC: *Brig J M Hamilton*	GOC: *Brig A C Hughs*	18, 24,68/Field Regiments
1/Oxfordshire & Bucks Light Infantry	2/ Royal Warwicks	2/Gloucesters	53/Anti-Tank Regiment
1/7 Royal Warwicks	5/ Gloucesters	4/ Oxfordshire & Bucks Light Infantry	**Royal Engineers**
8/ Royal Warwicks	8/ Worcesters	1/Buckinghamshire Battalion (Ox & Bucks)	9, 224, 226/Field Companies
			227/Field Park Company

II Corps
GOC: Lieutenant General Alan Brooke

Corps Troops

Infantry	Royal Artillery	Royal Engineers
2/Royal Northumberland Fusiliers (4th Division)	60, 88/Field Regiments	222, 234, 226/Field companies
2/Middlesex (3rd Division)	53, 59/Medium Regiments	108/Corps Field Park
1/7 Middlesex	53/Light Anti-Tank Regiment	14/Corps Field Survey Company
	2/Survey Regiment	

1st Division (With II Corps from 18-23 May)
GOC: Major General the Hon Harold Alexander

1 (Guards) Brigade	2 Brigade	3 Brigade	Artillery
GOC: *Brig Merton Beckwith-Smith*	GOC *Brig Charles Hudson VC*	GOC: *Brig Thomas Wilson*	2,19,67/Field Regiments
3/Grenadier Guards	1/Loyal Regiment	1/Duke of Wellingtons	21/Anti-Tank Regiment
2/Coldstream Guards	2/North Staffords	2/Sherwood Foresters	**Royal Engineers**
2/Hampshires	6/Gordon Highlanders	1/Kings Shropshire Light Infantry	23, 238, 248/Field Companies
			6/Field Park Company

3rd Division
GOC: Major General Bernard Law Montgomery

7 (Guards) Brigade	8 Brigade	9 Brigade	Artillery
GOC: *Brig John Whitaker*	GOC: *Brig Christopher Woolner*	GOC: *Brig William Robb*	7, 33, 76/ Field Regiment
1/Grenadier Guards	1/ Suffolks	2/ Lincolnshire Regiment	20/Anti-Tank Regiment
2/Grenadier Guards	2/The East Yorkshires	1/The King's Own Scottish Borderers	**Royal Engineers**
1/Coldstream Guards	4/ Royal Berkshires	2/The Royal Ulster Rifles	17, 246, 253/Field Companies
			15/Field Park Company

III Corps
GOC: Lieutenant General Sir Ronald Adam (to 26 May) Major General S R Watson

Corps Troops

Infantry	Artillery	Royal Engineers
1/9 Manchesters (with 5th Division from 14 May)	5/RHA	214, 217/Field Companies
	97/ Field Regiment	293/Corps Field Park
	56/Medium Regiment	514 Corps Field Survey Company
	54/Light Anti-Aircraft Regiment	
	3/Survey Regiment	

4th Division (With III Corps 18-23 May)
GOC: Major General Dudley Graham Johnson VC

10 Brigade	11 Brigade	12 Brigade	Artillery
GOC: *Brig Evelyn Barker*	GOC: *Brig Kenneth Anderson*	GOC: *Brig K L Hawkesworth*	22, 30, 77/Field Regiments
2/ Bedfordshire & Herts	2/ Lancashire Regiment	2/The Royal Fusiliers	14/Anti-Tank Regiment
2/ Duke of Cornwall's Light Infantry	1/The East Surrey	1/South Lancashire	**Royal Engineers**
1/6 East Surrey	5/ Northamptonshire	6/The Black Watch	7, 59, 225/Field Companies
			18/Field Park Company

44th (Home Counties) Division
GOC: Major General E A Osborne

131 Brigade	132 Brigade	133 Brigade	Artillery
GOC: *Brig John Utterson-Kelso*	GOC: *Brig James Steele*	GOC: *Brig Noel Whitty*	57,58,65/Field Regiments
2/Buffs (East Kent)	1/QORWK (Royal West Kent)	2/Royal Sussex	57 Anti-Tank Regiment
1/5 Queens Royal Regiment]	4/QORWK	4/Royal Sussex	**Royal Engineers**
1/6 Queens Royal Regiment	5/QORWK	5/Royal Sussex	11, 208, 210/Field Companies
			211/Field Park Company

Selected Bibliography

The National Archives
Unit War Diaries in WO 166 and 167.
Personal accounts in CAB 106 and WO 217.
POW Reports in WO 344, WO 373.

Imperial War Museum Sound Archive
West Sussex Record Office
King's College Archive
The RUSI Library

Published Sources
Blaxland, G, *Destination Dunkirk: The Story of Gort's Army*, William Kimber 1973.
Brooks, G, *Grand Party*, Hutchinson 1942.
Chaplin, H D, *Queen's Own Royal West Kent Regiment 1920-1950*, Michael Joseph 1954.
Cuncliffe, M, *History of the Royal Warwickshire Regiment 1919-1955*, Clowes 1956.
Daniell, D S, *Cap of Honour*, White Lion 1951.
The History of the East Surrey Regiment, Vol IV, Ernest Benn 1957.
Ellis, L, *The War in France and Flanders*, HMSO 1953.
Forbes, P, *The Grenadier Guards in the War of 1939-1945, Vol 1*, Gale and Polden 1949
Foster, R, *The History of The Queen's Royal Regiment Vol VIII 1924-1948*, Gale and Polden 1953
Goldsmith, R and Godfrey,E, *History of the Duke of Cornwall's Light Infantry 1939-1945,* Regimental History Committee 1966.
Howard, M, & Sparrow, J, *History of the Coldstream Guards 1920-46*, Oxford 1951.
Jackson, J, *The Fall of France,* OUP 2003.
Langley, J M, *Fight Another Day*, Collins 1974.
Neville, M C, *The Ox and Bucks Light Infantry Chronicle Vol 1*, Gale and Polden 1949.
Nicholson, W N, *The History of the Suffolk Regiment 1928-1946*, East Anglian Magazine 1948
Quilter, D C, *No Dishonourable Name*, William Cloves 1947.
Sebag-Montefiore, H, *Dunkirk – Fight to the Last Man*, Viking 2006.
Synge, W, *The Story of the Green Howards*, The Regiment 1954.
Thompson, J, *Dunkirk – Retreat To Victory*, Sidgwick and Jackson 2008.

Index

Adair, Maj A., 39–40, 112, 143
Adam, Lt Gen Sir R., 5, 12, 157
Ambrosius, *Hauptmann* L., 39, 133, 145
Anzegem, ix, 12, 71, 83
Army Group A, vii–ix, 7, 9–10
Army Group B, ix, 7
Avelgem, 28, 30, 65, 94–5, 98

Bailleul, 108, 112, 143, 145
Baker, Lt Col R., 50–3, 129, 131–5
Barclay, Capt P., 46–9, 121, 123–6
Barker, Brig E., 26, 28, 94, 158
Barker, Maj Gen M., 3, 44, 49, 156
Beckwith-Smith, Brig M., 35, 107–108, 157
Berchem, 20, 22, 88–9
Blanchard, Gen G., 7–9
Bléharies, vii, ix, 55, 57
Billotte, Gen G., 10
Birch, Lt Col J., 28–31, 93–6
Bock, *Generaloberst* F. von, 7
Bootle-Wilbraham, Lt Col L., 34, 37, 43, 104, 108, 110–11, 117
Boxshall, Lt Col R., 21–2, 24–5, 65
British Expeditionary Force (BEF):
Corps:
I Corps, 2–4, 9, 44, 46, 49, 51, 156
II Corps, 3–4, 32, 157
III Corps, 5, 12, 157
Divisions:
1st, 4, 8, 34, 45, 101, 104
2nd, 4, 44, 46, 60
3rd, 4, 8, 32, 101–102
4th, 4, 8, 12, 20, 88
42nd (East Lancashire), 5, 9, 44
44th (Home Counties), 5, 9, 12, 20, 22, 57, 71, 89
48th (South Midland), 5, 8, 44, 49
Brigades:
1/Armoured Reconnaissance, 3
1 Infantry, 35, 104
4 Infantry, 50, 121
6 Infantry, 44
7 Infantry, 32, 101–102
8 Infantry, 32–3, 102
9 Infantry, 32, 34,102
10 Infantry, 28
125 Infantry, 45–6
126 Infantry, 44
127 Infantry, 44
131 Infantry, 12, 15–16, 18, 80
132 Infantry, 12, 74, 76
133 Infantry, 12, 87
143 Infantry, 49, 129, 132, 152
144 Infantry, 49, 132, 151, 154
151 Infantry, 145
Regiments:
1/Border, 45–6, 119
1/Cameron Highlanders, 53–4, 137
1/Coldstream Guards, 33, 102
1/East Lancashire, 44
1/East Surrey, 20–1, 24, 65, 98
1/Grenadier Guards, 32–3
1/Loyals, 63
1/Ox and Bucks, 54, 120, 129, 137
1/Royal Scots, 49–51, 57, 62, 129–32, 136
1/RWK, 17, 73, 76, 81
1/5 Queens, 16–18, 64, 78, 81, 83
1/6 East Surreys, 26, 28, 89, 100
1/6 Lancashire Fusiliers, 46, 127
1/6 Queens, 14–15, 17–18, 80, 82–3, 118
1/7 Royal Warwicks, 50, 52, 119, 127, 129, 134
1/8 Lancashire Fusiliers, 46, 127
2/Beds and Herts, 26, 28, 94
2/Coldstream Guards, 34, 102, 104, 116–17
2/DCLI, 26, 92, 100
2/Essex, 65
2/Gloucesters, 55, 62
2/Grenadier Guards, 32–3, 63, 102, 114, 118–19
2/Hampshires, 104, 106, 109, 117
2/Lancashire Fusiliers, 21, 25–6, 63, 90, 93, 99

2/North Staffords, 35, 42–3, 113
2/Royal East Kent (Buffs), 14, 77, 79–80
2/Royal Norfolks, 46, 121, 127
2/Royal Sussex, 18, 20
2/Royal Warwicks, 50, 54–5, 61, 132, 137
3/Grenadier Guards, 35, 38, 43, 104, 117
4/Northumberland Fusiliers, 8
4/Ox and Bucks, 55–6
4/RWK, 13, 19–20, 73–5, 77, 86
5/Northamptons, 21, 23, 89
5/RWK, 19, 20, 72–3
6/Black Watch, 23, 90, 100
8/Royal Warwicks, 49, 51, 54, 121, 129, 131–2, 135
Royal Engineers:
7/Field Company, 21, 88
210/Field Company, 72, 74, 85–6
248/Field Company, 119
Artillery:
10/Field Regiment, 62, 64
18/Field Regiment, 62, 118
22/Field Regiment, 30, 98
52/Light Anti-Aircraft Regiment, 65
68/Field Regiment, 62, 136
115/Field Regiment, 62, 118
140/Field Regiment, 62–3, 136
Brooke, Lt Gen A., 2, 32, 58, 157
Bruyelle, 56, 62, 129, 132, 136–7

Calonne, 44, 46, 48, 50–1, 53, 55, 62, 118, 121, 129–34, 136
Canal d'Espierres, 102
Cemeteries:
  Anzegem Communal, 86–7
  Avelgem Communal, 100
  Bailleul Communal, 114–16
  Bruyelle War, 136–7
  Calonne Communal, 127–8, 135–6
  Chercq Churchyard, 122, 134
  Estaimbourg Churchyard, 117
  Esquelmes War, 113, 117–19, 134, 143
  Froyennes Communal, 119
  Helkijn Churchyard, 114–15
  Hollain Churchyard, 137, 149
  Ingoyghem Military, 99–100
  Kaster Churchyard, 98

  Moregem Churchyard, 86
  Oudenaarde Communal, 85
  Pecq Communal, 117
  Templeuve Communal, 119
  Tournai Communal Extension, 119–20
Chamberlain, N., 1
Château de Beauregard, 44
Château Bernard, 108–109, 139, 146
Château du Biez, 37, 105, 107–108
Château de Bourgogne, 35, 106–108
Château de Chartreaux, 46
Château de Curgies, 46–7, 121, 127–8
Château d'Espierres, 32, 104
Château de Lannoy, 53, 147, 152–3
Chercq, 44, 46, 121–2, 124, 127, 130, 134
Chief of The Imperial General Staff (CIGS), 2–3, 5, 11
Chitty, Lt Col A., 13–14, 20, 73, 75
Churchill, W.S., x, 10–11
Colvin, Maj R., 33–4, 102

Dill, Lt Gen Sir J., 2–3, 11
Domein de Ghellink, 82–4
Drinkwater, Gdsm L., 38–43, 113, 119, 141–2
Dunn, Lt Col P., 50–1, 147
Dyle, river, ix, 7–10

École Moyenne, 103–104, 106
Eine, viii–xi, 12–13, 71, 73
Elsegem Château *see* Kwaadestraat Château
Escanaffles, 27–30, 88, 92, 95–8
Estaimbourg, 35–7, 104–107
Esquelmes, 42, 113, 119, 145

Fall Gelb, 7
Froyennes, 44–5, 113–14

Gamelin, Gen M., 4, 6–8, 10–11
Gort, Viscount J,. vii, 1–6, 8, 10, 57–8, 156
Gort Line, 4, 26, 49
Green, Lt Col W., 21–4, 90
Gristock, CSM G., 48–9, 123–5

Helkijn, 32–3, 101–102
Holdich, Capt N., xii, 52–3, 131

Hollain, xii, 50, 61, 120, 132, 147–55
Holmes, Maj Gen W., 44, 156
Hore-Belisha, L., 1–2, 5
Horwood, Sgt A., 18–19
Huiwede, 15, 71, 78–81, 89–90

Ironside, Gen Sir E., 2–3

Johnson, Maj Gen D., 20, 158
Jollain-Merlin, 55

Kasteelwijk Château *see* Moregem Château
Kaster, 88
Kerkove, 20–1, 23–4, 88–90
Kwaadestraat Château, 14, 17–18, 71, 82
Knok, ix, 12, 71

Langley, Lt J., 35–6, 109–10, 138–9
Lasne, River, 9–10
Law, Lt Col H., 44–5, 114
Leggett, Pte E., 46–7, 49, 123–5
Lloyd, Lt Col J., 32, 102
Louvain, 7–8

Maginot Line, 4–6, 46, 58, 121
Marlborough, Duke of, x–xi
Manstein, *Generalletnant* E. von, 7
Mechelen Affair, 6–7
Meuse, River, ix, 9–10
Mole, Lt Col G., 50, 129
Money, Lt Col D., 49–50, 57, 62, 130–1, 133
Mont de l'Enclus, ix, 20–1, 26, 28, 88, 93, 95
Mont St Aubert, ix, 34, 140
Moregem, 73–4, 76
Moregem Château, 19, 74–7
Montgomery, Maj Gen B., 2–3, 32, 102, 157
Muirhead, Brig J., 129, 152, 157

Nicholls, Gdsm H., 40–2, 113–14, 145

Osborne, Lt Gen E., 12, 158
Oudenaarde, vii–xi, 9, 12, 14, 19–20, 57, 67–8, 71–4, 77, 81–2, 85–6, 88

Pecq, 34–6, 41, 101–102, 104, 108, 111, 117, 138–46
Petegem, 15–17, 64, 76–8, 80–1
Petegem Château *see* Scheldekant Château
Pont-a-Chin, 37, 50, 63, 104, 112–13
Poplar Ridge, 38–41, 112–13, 117, 138, 143–5

Reinberger, Maj H., 6
Rijtgracht, 26–7, 30, 90, 92–3, 95–6, 98, 100
Rougier, Lt Col L., 26, 90–1, 99
Rugge, 26–7, 92–4, 100
Runstedt, *Generaloberst* G. von, vii
Rushton, Lt Col E., 26, 28, 30, 92–3, 95
Ryder, Maj J., 48, 129

Tomes, Capt D., xii, 50–1, 54–5, 61, 147–51, 155
Tournai, viii, x–xii, 44–6, 49, 62, 65, 67–8, 101, 113–14, 120–1

Scheldekant Château, 15, 81–2
St Maur, 62–3, 118, 129, 132, 136
Sysonby, Maj Lord E., 16–17, 78

Utterson-Kelso, Brig J., 15, 80, 158

Visiting CWGC Cemeteries, 69–70

Waarmaarde, 91, 93
Waregem, 12, 87
Warnaffles Farm, 50, 53, 62, 67, 121, 129, 131–5
Whitaker, Brig J., 32, 157
Whitfield, Lt Col W., 151–2
Whitty, Brig N., 12, 158
Wild, Rev D., 55